Gods

Spoken Word

A HABAKKUK 2:3 STORY

Author Prophetess
Gwendolyn King

iUniverse, Inc.
New York   Bloomington

God's Spoken Word
A Habakkuk 2:3 Story

iUniverse books may be ordered through booksellers or by contacting:

iUniverse
1663 Liberty Drive
Bloomington, IN 47403
www.iuniverse.com
1-800-Authors (1-800-288-4677)

ISBN: 978-1-4502-7288-9 (pbk)
ISBN: 978-1-4502-7289-6 (cloth)
ISBN: 978-1-4502-7290-2 (ebk)

Printed in the United States of America

iUniverse rev. date: 11/3/2010

And the Lord said to me, write my answer on a billboard large and clear, so that anyone can read it at a glance and rush to tell others, but these things I plan won't happen right away, slowly, steadily and surely the time approaches when the vision will be fulfilled. If it seems slow, do not despair, for these things will surely come to pass. Just be patient! They will not be overdue a single day!

(L.B.V.)
Author Prophetess Gwendolyn King

Contents

Dedication ix

Acknowledgements xi

Introduction xiii

Chapter 1   God's Spoken Word: God's hand Is All Over Me 1

Chapter 2   Destiny Walk Begins. God's Spoken Word
God's Hand Is All Over Me 28

Chapter 3   Snatched into Purpose 47

Chapter 4 57

Prayer of Thanks 64

Prophetess Prayer 65

Prophetess Final Words 67

Prophetess Final Words 93

Dedication

I dedicate my book to my children and my family as well as every man, woman and child. That whatever God's word says we can do! We can do! *Philippians 4:13. We can do all things through Christ who gives us the strength!* All we have to do is walk with God's word out in the flesh with the spirit of faith that we serve the only one true living God. Know that Jesus' Victory lives deep inside each and every one of us. Though we have been tried as silver, God has brought us into a wealthy place (Psalms 66:10 – 12) and I prophetess Gwendolyn King Declare the Decree (Isaiah 48:3). I love you! God has the final word. I put no other Gods before him.

Acknowledgements

I couldn't do this without the Holy Spirit leading and guiding me through all the past hurts and abuse. Thank you Holy Spirit for your comfort! I'd like to acknowledge Sister Rhonda Smith who without her typing skills this book would not be written in God's timing. I'd like to thank my step-sister and her husband for all their help typing up my songs. Last and of course not least, my number one daughter for all her love and support; through it all, she has been my number one fan. She has helped me with a roof over my head and supplied so many spiritual needs, like standing in agreement when I had no one else to believe in and agree with me. She was there through all my mood swings, when the old me was being stripped away. I love and thank you. To my number one and only son, I thank him because whenever his mother needed some extra money to get her through, he was right there and sent it; however he had to do it, I got it. I love you and thank you so much. To my precious baby girl, the one I stuck with all those 101 names, I thank her for her steady, unconditional love. Thank you and God's Blessings always.

To my mother, sisters and brother, grand-baby Monique for believing in me, who pushed me to write my songs and encouraged me to have strength and write my autobiography, thank you.

Introduction

As long as I have walked with the Lord, I have done so practically all by myself, with only the power of the Holy Spirit to help me and to teach me the ways of God. I came to realize that the body of Christ (The Church) in this crucial time in our lives, when the world is spinning out of control in every area, is made manifest through his Son Jesus, who will soon return to the world. The Church needs to pray for wisdom and courage like we have never before, to obtain the knowledge of God on how to lead the lost to Jesus. We must cry out for sinners to accept and grow to know and love Jesus, as their Lord and personal Savior, who was slain for our sins, the Savior of the world. Thank you Jesus!

I don't want another soul to go through what I had to endure. I didn't have powerful men and women prophesying over me or speaking life into my spirit! It didn't happen for me like that! We as Pastors and Ministers of the Gospel, the good news, have to not only pray for the lost in Christ who want to know Jesus but don't know quite how to look for him or what steps to take. We the Church have to be made available to the drug addicts who need someone to walk it out with, when those withdraws come, and believe me, they will come. I know that when the withdraws do come, we the Church of Jesus will have to be there to help. As representative of Jesus in the earth, we have to address our own issues, because not all who claim a part of the body of Christ are being honest. There are some of us who have to deal with sex issues, those who masturbate, who still look at porno on the down low, as well as some of us who still walk in un-forgiveness because of past hurts, and don't know how to really love.

I thank God for this experience to be able to put my life on the altar of this book. It seemed like I was born to absorb all the bad elements of life. To live my experiences, and through my testimony, minister to a world of hurting people. I couldn't connect to Ministers or Pastors who hadn't actually experienced my kind of pain. I thank the Lord for every test and trial that allows me to use my misery as my ministry. The Lords Kingdom shall be established and his people shall be redeemed out of the hands of the enemy in the name of Jesus (Psalms 107:2).

The Lord spoke to me and said this book is the weapon I want you to use to defeat the enemy in this hour. Moses had a shudder and a rod. King David had five smooth stones and King Solomon had the wisdom of God; Prophetess Gwendolyn has her book, Bless God!

You are one of my Heavy Weight Contenders of the faith that I saved for last. Thank you Jesus! I know now that Jesus can't deliver everyone when we want him to, some of us have to have a Lazarus experience (St. John 11 :4). It's not that he doesn't love us. It's all for the Glory of God, that when we receive our healing and deliverance, the world will know that it was nobody but God.

If this book does well or doesn't, my life has been all for the Glory of God. With each experience, I fell in love with Jesus over and over again. Through my trying times I wrote songs of praise and redemption! Without those Songs that were given to me by the Holy Spirit, I don't think I would have made it through my valleys, to stand on the mountaintop of God's goodness to prophesy to his people. There was a time when my life was built on nothing but Jesus blood and righteousness, because he staked his life on it!

There came a time in my life when I had to believe in the living God. He was the only God I knew. He is perfect; there could be no other God for me. Every word of the Bible spoken over me shall come to pass, because his word can't come back void. The third Song was dedicated to the Lord because I love him. He is truly my hero; I couldn't have known him or feel the power of his might, if I never experienced struggles and trials. Please enjoy the songs that are at the end of this book. I know the words will surely bless you.

May the Peace of our Lord be with you always, I love you!

Prophetess Gwendolyn King.

Autobiography of Gwendolyn King
November 20, 1960 – Rapture
Ephesians 4:11 – 12

God sent apostles, prophets, evangelists, pastors and teachers to perfect me to perform the work of the ministry – edifying humanity to the goodness and greatness of the body of Christ.

This book is about the influence of God's word over one woman's life. Although she faced adversity and severe heartbreak in her life, her faith maintained her and God's word stood up triumphant. What the world and Satan placed in her path for her destruction, God intervened and turned it around for her good. Those who schemed plotted and devised evil plans fell under submission to God's glory.

This book is about God's redeeming power. How Jesus loved and saved me, how he delivered me, no mater where in life I stood – in clubs or walking the streets, in or out of a bad relationship. God's word hovered over me, and at the appointed time, he released the shackles of every hindering situation, and at the due season, gave me power over pain, strength to persevere, and wisdom to witness to non-believers.

Habakkuk 2:3 is about faith; it's a lesson about the lifestyle God's people must follow. *For the just, God's people shall live by faith.* It is about God's due season, his ultimate plan for our lives that he has set in place. No one knows that time but God, and until that time comes, we must live by faith that God's due season shall surely come, and won't be a moment late.

To be a child of God, you must be washed in the blood of the lamb. To be free of the burdens of sin, you must conquer the tests that face you, and stay true to the word of God. Christians must remain resolute thorough the tough times, by faith, every battle we fight has already been won by the blood our Lord and Precious Savior, King Jesus Christ shed on the cross. *2Corinthians 12:9* God's grace is more than sufficient to overcome any addiction and bad relationship we ever encountered. God's grace is more than sufficient to forgive anyone that harmed us in anyway. God's grace is more than sufficient to lead us in pursuing his purpose. When God's people come into the full understanding of who they are and whom they serve, that we will go through much spiritual warfare, that with a mature spiritual sense of knowledge realizes that this world is not our home, that we are souls passing through to a higher calling, then the things of the flesh will fail to phase, manipulate or entice the people of God, to live a defeated life.

This is an amazing Prophetic love story between one woman and her Lord. That Jesus' Christ victory does live in the lives of His people, and what God has done for one woman he can do for another. This book is the author's testimony of God's Grace.

Prophetess Gwendolyn King although faced with enormous adversity in life, was given an awesome anointed mantle of prophetess on her life, not of her choice, but by God himself, to overcome any and every obstacle set before her. God has given her his grace to pursue his purpose and his plan for her life, to advance his kingdom at all costs necessary.

Prophetess Gwendolyn King is founder of God's Precious Kingdom Ministries in association with Chosen and K.I.R. "Keep it Real With Jesus and Company". She has three children and one granddaughter and a host of friends and family that support her and her vision as she goes forth proclaiming "Jesus' Victory".

CHAPTER 1

God's Spoken Word: God's hand Is All Over Me

On November 20, 1960, Gwendolyn Nicholson named after the one and only great Black poet Gwendolyn Brooks, was born to Otis and Lee Vera Nicholson, in the very small town of Parkdale in Ashley County, Arkansas. The baby was delivered by a midwife, who was known for her special gifts. Some say she was a soothe sayer, which was really nothing unusual. Many people had those types of gifts who practiced in voodoo and witch crafts of all sorts, which still goes on a lot today in the South.

As I look back over my life, I believe at that very moment when I took my first breath of life, I began God's Spoken Word. It was as though he was saying this is my anointed Prophet, who would have to overcome much. Who would have known my misery would become my ministry? I know now that God made it, so that I can be used for his Glory.

By no means did being chosen by God mean I was going to have a carefree life. Instead, it was a life of abuse of all kinds, shapes and forms. A father and mother that fought a lot, a father who was a very jealous, mean man. So jealous, that one rainy day, he hid outside a local cafe where my mother was a waitress. It so happens, thank God, my mother didn't work on that particular day. A woman who sort of looked liked my mother from what my Aunt had told us, came out of the cafe, and because of mistaken identity, was severely beaten with a baseball bat by my father. Shortly after my mother found out about the incident, she made arrangements to flee the South and headed North. I was three years old at the time. My younger brother was one, and my two sisters were six months and six years old, respectively. My baby sister of six months was too sick to travel and had to stay in Arkansas because of a severe case of pneumonia. My oldest sister was in school at the time my mother had to flee for her life. Later my mother sent for her, but my baby sister was never returned; my Aunt and Uncle didn't want to give her back. I believe they had a hidden agenda, and to this day there are a lot of unsaid words about that whole ordeal. My sister very seldom speaks to me. I believe it's because she feels cheated out of a mother that I had all my life and she didn't. Years later, I believe I was about six years old, we returned to my home town in Arkansas for visits and summer vacation

Those trips were very trying and dangerous at times because of the racism that strongly existed in those days. I remember my uncle being pulled over in the wee hours of the morning. The drive to our hometown takes about sixteen hours straight through. I was awakened by flashlights in my face and the loud voices of white police officers yelling at my Uncle who always drove us down home.

"Step out the car boy!"

"What's your name boy!"

"Is this your car boy?"

Then they would direct their yelling to my mother.

"What's your name gal? Are these your children?!"

This was my first experience with racism. I was so scared; my heart felt like it was beating out of my chest. We continued going to Arkansas for visits every summer and holidays. I especially loved going to Church with my Aunt who was very active in the Church of God in Christ. I believe I fell in love with Jesus at the young age of six. I wanted to know this awesome man who everybody gets so dressed up to go see that people would cry about, jump, holler and fall out all over the floor, and in my Aunt's case, spent a lot of time with. I now know why she spent so much of her time with Jesus. Having an alcoholic husband and raising nine children, she had to stay in prayer and fellowship with God. I wanted everybody to know Jesus. I began evangelizing at the age of nine years old. I'd go up to other children and ask them if they wanted to know Jesus and if they would come to Church with me. Some did and of course some didn't. I believe that year I began to hear the Lords voice as I continued to evangelize and witness for him.

I loved my summer vacations to Arkansas. I spent time playing on the dusty red dirt roads with my cousins, picking peaches, plums and mulberries off the trees – sweet memories, as well as feeding our chickens and pigs. I really miss hanging laundry on the outdoor clothes line.

One afternoon I was sitting on the couch watching television and my grandmother told me several times to go out and get the clothes off the clothes line. Because I figured she was old and that she would forget she even asked me, I pretended I didn't hear her. Let's just say that my family was very big disciplinarians. She took a wet dish cloth and went straight across my face with it. I laugh now, but at that moment in time, "Wow" I was shocked. Best believe I never underestimated her being old or forgetful again. I loved my granny. She is now deceased.

My grandmother taught me so much. She showed me how to grow and can, to put up my own vegetables, as well as how to survive hard times. I enjoyed my grandmother's stories of when she had to pick cotton and tomatoes for a living. Granny had so many stories to tell. I especially enjoyed the story about the house she lived in, and how it was a Chinese boot camp, and that at times she could hear chains rattling of the captured prisoners.

As a child that house seemed very creepy and scary to me. My family still owns that property today. I used to walk by the house when I was a child very quickly, looking up at it as it stood on big cement blocks as so many of the old houses did in those days. They had tin roofs, and at bed time if it was raining, the sound of the rain hitting the tin roof would put me to sleep. Now that was some good sleep.

The only part of summer I hated was the end, which meant I was going back to Illinois. It's the place where I was sexually molested by an older female friend of the family, who would babysit us when my mother had to work or went out to party with friends. If that wasn't enough, I had to go home to a town that was mostly white dominated and very narrow minded, set in old racist ways. I never mentioned the molestation to anyone. I think at the age of nine years old I really didn't understand what was happening. I just knew it made me uncomfortable.

Back then, children were seen and not heard, I didn't have a lot of opinions or choices, so I went to school as usual. Going to school from first grade through third grade in the North wasn't so bad. I went to school with most of the kids from my neighborhood, mostly people of color, Blacks, Latinos and a few lower class whites, we all knew each other. We would go to each others' houses and play baseball in the backyard; we all got along well. However, going to school became an ordeal when things began to change.

In 1969 and 1970, new middle class schools were built. A lot of children were bussed out of our neighborhood to the upper middle white area of town. My life would never be the same (God's hand Is All Over Me). When I tried to fit in with the rich white kids, I got called nigger and when I went home to the neighborhood, I got called Uncle Tom by the black kids. It seemed like I couldn't win, so I pretty much stayed to myself, no real special click to speak of. Eventually, I befriended some rich doctor's kids and I began to stay at their house overnight. Of course the black kids in the neighborhood hated it, and it seemed like every time I peeked my head out, I had to fight or be called Uncle Tom or honky lover. It wasn't until I got to my Junior High school that things got back to somewhat normal.

Returning to school in the neighborhood, I found kids I was comfortable with, who I could hang out and am myself with. They were the white hippies, the cigarette smokers, the beer drinkers and the party all the time 'weed heads'. We would meet up every morning at our smoke corner which was located across from the school, for our morning cigarettes and our drug exchange. Our weekends were the highlight of our lives, it consisted of a hog roast and live bands. Life was exciting or so we thought, and they liked me, even though I was black. To be honest, I think they stayed so high they really didn't care or thought much about it. Besides, I supplied the weed and brought it to school and they paid me for it. So if they used me I used them as well, it just worked. I remember a time when I was making a drug sell behind the school and they wanted to try the weed, so we lit up a joint. As I was about to hand the joint over, there was a teacher looking right in my face. I'd say I was "busted" not only with the weed; I also had an illegal 7" inch switch blade with me.

I just got that stash of weed the night before from one of my good guy friends that was down visiting from Minneapolis, Minnesota. I was kind of fly then, not a bad looking girl. I had my way with the black guys and the white guys. I got in so much trouble that day, but the person who got hurt the most was my mother. It killed a little something in me when I saw the look on her face when they released me into her custody.

You see, I knew what my mother had to go through to raise us – the racism and abuse she endured from my father. For me to add another worry to what she endured bothered me a lot. You would think after all that I would've stopped causing her pain, not! That was just the beginning. (God's hand Is All Over Me.)

Going to School in the 1970s with the Vietnam War and racism all up in your face everyday was a trying experience. We had racial riots at school, which at times would go on for weeks. Somebody was always starting a fight after school. So when the riots were going on I had to live a split life. I had to be there to ride or die with the blacks. During down times when the riots began to calm down, I'd get back with my white hippy friends and we would kick it and get our party on. There were a lot of parties in those days; the blacks in the hood would throw parties especially at the local college. There was a lot of sexual activity going on all around. I did however manage to keep my virginity for the most part of my early years, up to16 years old, woo! I remember crashing our boring school dances and making them what I thought livelier, selling some of the rich white kids weed and pills that they normally wouldn't know where to get. I began to skip school more and hangout with friends whose parents worked during school hours; we just sat around smoking weed and making plans for the weekend, trying to figure out whose handwriting was good enough to write an absent note from school the next day. I believe we stayed high to forget the ugliness that existed in our lives at that time.

This went on most of junior high school. (God's plan is always at work) I didn't stay in high school much. I started going to a lot of house parties in the neighborhood, hanging out with my homies. I started dating a black basketball player. One night, my boyfriend, his sister, her boyfriend and I went to a party. Afterward, we all left in my boyfriend's sister's so called boyfriend's car. He dropped my boyfriend and his sister off first and decided to drop me off last. I was feeling kind of funny but didn't pay a lot of attention to it at first. I was still in the back seat where my boyfriend and I sat. I happened to notice that he passed my house and went way out to the boonies. That's where my neighborhood was, in the boondocks. I'm like, 'hey you passed my house', he said 'I know'. He pulled over in a secluded area, stopped the car, got in the backseat and tried to rape me. I couldn't believe it. We just had a good time with the people we supposedly loved and here he is trying to rape me?

When I pushed him off of me he said 'if you don't give me some I'm making you walk home naked'. I said 'bet! I'd rather walk home naked then'. Until this day, I believe God stepped in; the guy got out of the backseat of the car and drove me home. I never told anyone, I just tried not to think about it. That year I dropped out of high school and left the neighborhood to go live with my uncle William, my Mother's half brother. He was cool as heck. We drank together, smoked weed, we just kicked it. He took me fishing. He was like the dad I never had. I was so glad he was in my life. He had a girlfriend who had three children. They lived in the area projects.

At that time, I thought life was very good. Now I know that I was just trying to bury all the hurt I had accumulated in such a short time of life. I'm now 16 years old and I met a whole new group of people (God's hand Is All Over Me). They were poor like me and loved to party. At that time in my life, that's what was up. I tried to stay as numb as possible and not think of all the crap that was going on, that I had been through. I was the girl in the projects that had the uncle with the good weed and he hooked me up on the weed tip.

I sold weed in massive quantities, balling! If you wanted the good stuff you knew I was the girl to see. This went on for quite some time, up until my uncle took very sick. He contracted lung cancer at a local coal factory where he worked for years. He died that summer of 1976. We were devastated by his death, but instead of sitting around after his funeral feeling all sad and depressed, we partied and threw the biggest party, which lasted for days! We had all kinds of people coming in and out. There was this one especially cute guy I noticed, who I had never seen before. He was a fine Latin brother who had just moved into the projects. He became my first love, the one I gave my virginity to. Who would have known that our love would last off and on for another decade?

Shortly after I lost my virginity, his mother had to move back to their hometown. We did manage to stay in touch. His sister became one of my best friends. I can honestly say I believe my first love and his sister were my only true best friends throughout my whole life. They used to come down to visit me during the Christmas Holiday Season. My family seemed to really like them, unlike any of my other weed head friends. I guess it was because when they were there I would stay home more, but as soon as they'd leave I would be back to the street. After my uncle's death, selling weed went under, but we continued to party like there was no tomorrow. School was about to start back up and summer was officially over, it seemed like everybody but me, was going back to school.

I eventually left my Aunt's house in the projects and went back home to my mother's, only to find my mother had a new boyfriend who without giving him a chance, I decided I didn't like him. I ran away from home at the age of sixteen with some gang members from the LLK, headed to Chicago. On our way to Chicago, we got pulled over by the police for a broken taillight and when asked our names, they soon found out I was a run away and my mother was looking for me; so they took me to the Pontiac Jail near Chicago IL. I was later released to my mother. Her boyfriend who I didn't like was there. That was the longest ride home I ever took.

Later as time went on he began to grow on me. I guess it was because he tried to buy me and it worked. What sixteen year old girls do you know who don't like to shop? Not only that, I now have what every child wants, a two parent home. He took us on vacation all over the United States and even some parts of Canada. I thought that was so awesome, but the most important thing he did for me was take us to Arkansas every year. Going home meant so much to me – it was where I could find my roots when things were spinning out of control in the North. I could go home where I knew I could feel Jesus. Going to Church with my Auntie seemed so peaceful, and seeing my family was real special.

When I got back home from Arkansas that year 1978, I decided it was time for me to get a job and move out of my mother's house. My brother and sister were gone to college; it was time for me to leave as well. I didn't want to go back to school and collect my dead father's social security. I figured he didn't want to help me when he was living so why would he willingly want to help me now that he's dead. I got a job at the local college in the kitchen, moved into my first apartment and later started dating again. He wasn't Mexican like my first love, he was a Black guy from the rival school we attended when we were younger. Only Blacks from the right side of the tracks and upper class Whites went to his school. Who would've thought he and I would even hook up? (God's hand Is All Over Me)

My boyfriend and I did everything together. We took trips and did a lot of babysitting for one of my older cousins. She had two boys, a bad marriage and a temper. I've seen throwing a butcher knife at her husband like it was nothing. They fought like that all the time. Now that's what you call good ole country fighting. My mother told me a story once that when her brother and sister were young, (now remember I told you my family were big disciplinarians, but to me this was capital punishment "Hello"), my grandmother would get those big potato crocus sacks, put them in it, would hang them up on a clothes line and beat them like old dusty rugs. That was just mean, but that's how the older family members got down in them days. My older cousin must have picked up that family mean streak, she surely kept her husband ducking and dodging all the time. Look back to that time I kind of chuckle to myself and think "Wow", I actually witnessed that. My cousin and her husband eventually divorced and she began to date; she was a very beautiful woman and had her way with the men. I'd say that the majority of the woman in my family did, including me.

My cousin worked at a local factory and made really good money. She was a professional thief and taught me how to be the best ("God hand is all over me"). We went from city to city taking pretty much what we wanted – the finest jewelry, expensive clothing, top of the line perfumes. We loved the lavish lifestyle – fancy cars and being some of best dress females; that was the lifestyle many of the females in our family lived, from Arkansas, Kansas City to Detroit, Michigan. Other females really couldn't stand us, we didn't care. My cousin and I never got caught; she did however remarry after her oldest son came back from boot camp and died of spinal meningitis at the age of sixteen. We were all devastated. At that time, he was one of the youngest in the family to die. His funeral was one of the biggest funerals I'd ever seen.

My cousin belonged to a very large motor cycle race club and every summer would hold motor cycle races and barbecues. The motor cycle club was very well known all over Illinois and Iowa. They came the day of my cousin's son's funeral from all over, to show their love and support. His death was a shock to us. I believe my cousin suffered a mental breakdown; some of her zest for life was gone. Her joy in the morning came when she met a wonderful man. Surprisingly he was white, a Lieutenant Colonel in the U S Army. They got married shortly after they met and moved away. I was happy for her and oh yeah he got a chance to experience her very well known country temper, just like her first husband had.

This husband was different; he loved her and could handle her. He brought her a lot of things, like a brand new little red sports car. I was at their house the day he gave it to her. Parked outside in the driveway all nice and shiny with a big red bow on it was an awesome little red car. What a Valentine's Day present! After my wild cousin settled down in her marriage and moved away, my life slowed down as well. I became pregnant with my first child in November of 1980.

At first life was good between my child's father and me. As my baby bump grew, he began to cheat. I found out in my ninth month about a girl and where she lived. With my big pregnant belly, I went over to her house and climbed some steep steps to her front door. Her door was open, I walked in and smacked her right in the face and walked out; my hormones were seriously out of whack. That was my first pregnancy so anything could happen right? On August 13, 1981 at 6:01 pm on a Thursday evening, I gave birth to a beautiful baby girl, life was back on track. We had our family and my child's father had decided to return to college that September to make a better life, so he said. I found out he cheated in college as well. What was I supposed to do? I had a baby now and I couldn't very well go back to being a professional thief. I didn't want to leave my child's father, because he promised to take good care of us.

Further, he was an investment that I intended to collect on, so I held it down as I best as I could. This was where my first struggle really began, when I became responsible for my child. ("God's hand Is All Over Me"). My daughter's father wasn't bringing in any money, I had to go on welfare for a while in order to have pampers and for my child to get food and proper medical. As I waited for my child's father to hold fast to that promise for a better life for us, I struggled with going out and getting a job. I'm used to working, but I had no one in my family to care for my child and I wasn't about to trust a stranger because of what happened to me when I was a child. Daycare was a no as well; my daughter was too young and could not talk. My child's father finally finished school, got a job, not a job he went to school for not right away, but a job to pay bills to support his family.

In 1982 when my daughter was two I decided to go back to school to get my GED and CNA Certificate. I promised myself I would return to school after my baby was potty trained and her father could help out with childcare, so I went back to school in order to get a better job and stop the struggle. Well that didn't last long, because I had to deal with a jealous baby daddy; he really had a lot of nerve after all the cheating he did. He actually stood outside the school I attended and waited for me to come outside. Just like my jealous father, he hid and spied on me while I was talking to a fellow male student about an assignment.

When I got home I got beat for it and that was the end of school for me. After me and my child's father got into that big fight, I got real tired of him – all the spying and acting a real nut. The feelings I had for him were gone. I went back to school and received my nursing certificate and got a job at a local nursing home. I enjoyed my job and the older people. I liked hearing their stories about their lives, past, present and about their families. I worked a third shift from 10:00pm to 6am that was an awesome shift; I was able to see the beautiful sunrise. That year I began to hang out with some of my Mexican girl friends, on my day off we would drive to a nearby town where the bars didn't close until 4am. As always, I was in charge of getting the weed to smoke on our way there. I guess it was to take the edge off.

Once I got pulled over for speeding. I hadn't been drinking, but I did have a beer before we left the house. The officer had me step out of the car to do a breath test. I didn't know what to expect from those types of tests, but there is one thing I knew when I passed that breath test, God's Hand Was all over me. I became a groupie of a local band that played every weekend and throughout the week; of course they were some very attractive Mexicans, my Latino brothers, woooooh!

We had so much fun after they finished playing for the night. We would go eat at one of the late night Mexican restaurants where they served authentic south of the border food where the atmosphere was like we stepped right into Mexico. "Yeah that's what was up", each of my girl friends had a guy in the band that she liked, I thought I'd grab me one as well; besides, my child's father was doing all the cheating in the relationship, I thought it was my turn. My daughter was now about five years old and she loved being at home with her daddy, so I took advantage of that situation. My girl friends and I had to play this game just right or we would get caught, and one of my friends was married.

I pretended I was going to work on my day off and hid my clothes I'll wear to the club in the bushes while my daughter's father was at work, he worked 1st shift. I would leave the house at 9:30pm, my shift started at 10:00pm, grabbed my clothes, drove my car to the nursing home and parked it like I was at work, in case Mister wanted to hide and sneak a peek, as to whether I was at work. One of my girlfriends would pick me up, and off we went to kick it with the band. One night we started having so much fun, the time got away from us. To be honest, we didn't care, I especially didn't. I thought it was time for him to find out, since obviously I was better at cheating than he was. This went on for years and he never found out until a night my friend and I said forget it, let's have the best time ever because we were already late to get back home. It was like 1 am and the club closed at 4am. Well all hell broke out, my married friend's husband called my child's father and they teamed up with both our daughters.

She had a little girl about the same age as my daughter. Those two men searched that little town not knowing we were nowhere in town. Words from my wise mother, never do your dirt where you lay your head. So with both of us M.I.A, I'd say we were pretty much "busted". We eventually ran across both of them. My girlfriend and I looked at each other with a 'your butt is in serious hot water look'. Although I cussed back then, I no longer curse or write cuss words, I'm a Christian, but I think you feel me about what I mean with us being in trouble. As we left to go home I said to her, 'if you don't hear from me in two hours, he has killed me.' We both laughed, but I was serious.

Well after that episode, he and I broke up for good. We fought that day. This time, he wasn't the only one throwing punches. I was making my own money, I moved out, got me a duplex house and started dating again and having fun. I ran across an old friend who I knew in school – of course he was Mexican. We were really good friends, he had been serving in the Army for ten years. We enjoyed each other's company; we shared some special times together that I will never forget. The laughter I once shared with my child's father, I now share with someone else and it was genuine. We fell in love that summer of 1985, spending all of his 30 day R and R (rest and relaxation) from the Army together. We had so much fun; we went to a little fair in a nearby town. My five year old really enjoyed the rides and she liked my friend even though he was not her father. He was just a likable person period.

At the end of our date my friend dropped us off as he usually did. When my daughter and I opened the front door, our home smelled like bacon had been cooking, as though someone came and made themselves at home without permission, and that person was still there. (God's hand Is All Over Me.) Now this could have turned out really bad, because in them days being single and living alone, believe me, a sister had access to a 25 caliber pistol. It turned out to be my child's father, who broke into my house while I was on my date and made himself at home. I found it real strange because he and I lost contact for a while. He must have been asking questions about where I lived and who I was dating, because he surely found me and had the nerve to cook my food.

I couldn't believe he was behind my door hiding and peeking. He was just a creep. I remember just sitting in my living on hot summer nights watching television and talking to my daughter, and he would just bust out and start talking out of nowhere, scaring the crap out of us. He did that crazy stuff more than once, even when I had company over. It was a real strange time in my life. I eventually moved from there. I couldn't take that weird crazy stuff anymore and I wasn't going to live my life all shut up in the house. My summer love ended, my boyfriend had to return his ARMY base, R and R was now officially over. We kept in touch for awhile, until he too became jealous. What gives with these men? He acted like I didn't have a life, just supposed to sit around the house waiting for his phone calls. Back in those days we didn't have cell phones or at least I should say I didn't. I believe cell phones didn't come out until 1987 or possibly 1988 not real sure.

My Army friend would call me from time to time from Germany and all over. There was a time I wasn't home and he left a message stating when he would call again, and if I wasn't home he would never call again. Well guess what? He called, I wasn't home, and he never called again. He didn't say a time and I stayed home that day for a long time. I finally decided to leave and take my daughter to visit some of her friends from the old neighborhood. He called me while we were out. Go figure that. Well he never called again. I was real hurt behind that, but you can't keep a good woman down.

In 1985 I was 25.years old; I decided I had my share with men and wanted a new direction in my life. My daughter and I joined the Church of God in Christ, which by the way is the same denomination as my home town church in Arkansas, so we fitted right in. Tired of all of the craziness that kept happening in my life; the drinking, parties and men coming and going out of my life – it was as though my spirit was crying out for help. There was an empty space in my soul that needed to be filled; I believe that's when my walk with Jesus as a grown woman began. ("God's Hand Is All Over me") My daughter and I came to love that little store front church. We met some really awesome people. The Pastor and his wife were so down to earth; they reminded me of some of my family down in Arkansas. I became the youth Sunday School Teacher, I sang in the choir as well as YPWW youth teacher, and later wrote and directed short plays and skits for the glory of God. I served that church for over twenty years.

The summer of 1985 brought many changes to my life; I remember it like it was yesterday. I still struggled with cigarettes and enjoyed a drink every now then – just keeping it real didn't mean I didn't love the Lord. Our church really didn't preach deliverance back then; they were more concerned about what you wore. You couldn't wear pants, makeup, or show your feet or toes, they were real big on the outer man, and how the outer man was suppose to look. In the meantime, your inner self is on a slow ride to hell, deteriorating from the lack of knowledge that guides you towards a personal relationship with Jesus. The religion aspect didn't work for me. ("God's hand Is All Over Me.") I became rebellious, my spirit didn't sit too well with 'no women can preach', and the whole pants thing just wore on me; but I didn't leave the church, I hung in there. Seeking Christ and not getting total deliverance because the Holy Spirit is absent from your Church can destroy a Christian. In fact, I drank and smoked weed even more.

In 1988, I began to try other drugs and stepped it up a bit with crack cocaine. One night as I was coming home from a party, on the way to my apartment, a man I had known from way back came out of nowhere and asked me had I ever tried crack before? My response was nope, but I will, so I tried it. I really didn't see the big deal, I didn't feel any different, no real big bang like everybody had said you would get, and that was that for now. Later that year, I started dating my daughter's father's cousin, his first cousin, two sister's children. We were cool with it, besides he wasn't my cousin, what did I care. We had fun together, traveled a lot and went to parties together. He had a really good job at a local steel factory, so every payday it was on. I ended up getting pregnant and that's when our relationship went down, everything between us went sour. He didn't believe the baby was his, which was a serious blow to me.

I continued to work for awhile then it got hard to hang on to my job. My baby's father was a closet crack addict, so more than once he kept my car out way pass time for me to be at work. Finally, after coming to work late or not showing up at all I got fired, and collected unemployment for awhile. Carrying this child was very difficult and his addiction was getting worse. My first child was eight years old when I became pregnant; I had given all of her things away, so I had nothing for this child. He took my income tax money that I was saving to buy things for my baby and spent it on drugs. He was just a lousy man and a father to be. Most men pamper their women when they are pregnant, he couldn't even buy me a fish sandwich that I had been craving. As a matter of fact, he never went out of his way for me and began to cheat as well. Wow I sure can pick them!? ("God's hand Is All Over Me")

Unlike my first pregnancy, this one was stressful – my boyfriend and I argued the entire time and eventually broke up towards the end. Shortly after, my Obstetrician diagnosed me with Placenta Abruptio, the placenta began detaching from my uterus. To save my baby, an emergency cesarean section was necessary. On Tuesday August 22, 1989 at 8:20am, I gave birth to a very handsome baby boy, a son, "that's alright" he was truly a blessing. His father and I got back together for a little while, but things really didn't improve - he continued to smoke crack and I eventually started to smoke with him. I guess I figured if you can't beat him join him. I don't know what I was thinking, and at that time I did not get hooked, I could take crack or leave it.

After years of on and off relationships, we decided to settle down and get married. All of the necessary preparations were made, the reception hall reserved, everything was going well, until one day when were both smoking, and by the way, I'm starting to like crack. Perhaps it was because my son's father was smoking openly in our house instead of hiding like he used to, but now I'm beginning to like crack a lot. One night as we were smoking we got into a big big argument about money and crack. Looking back, that episode kind of reminded me of a scene in the movie 'New Jack City', when the two crack heads were fighting. The girl used to be a prom queen, and a powerful drug like crack changed her from prom queen into a crack fiend. I have to take a moment to give God praise I love you Jesus - Thank you Jesus! ("God's hand Is All Over Me.")

Like the couple in that movie who were arguing over crack, our addiction was getting worse and controlling us. I went from smoking every payday to every time I felt the need. My son was about two years old then. Even though I'm smoking more and going out more, I'm not leaving my children with just anyone if they weren't going to be properly cared for. That usually meant my ten year old daughter is doing a lot of babysitting.

My mother bought a big duplex down the street from where she lived and moved us in, now it's on. A down the street baby sitter – I started going out more and more. Without realizing it, my mother was an enabler to my addiction. The relationship with my son's father was out of control; we smoked like we were crazy. When I didn't have money, I used my looks to get what I wanted. If a drug dealer wanted to date me, he had to pay it in exchange for whatever drug I wanted. I remember having multiple sex partners in one night and becoming pregnant ("God's grace as I write"). I didn't know who the father was. My son's father wanted it and thought the baby was his. He begged and begged me not to abort it, but I didn't listen. I went to a local abortion clinic and I aborted that baby for a selfish reason, I didn't want to stop smoking or partying ("Thank you Father for your mercy!")

The dysfunctional relationship with my son's father continued. We moved back in together promising to put the abortion behind us. Smoking crack was the one constant in our lives. Within weeks of the abortion I became pregnant again. Now this was crazy to me. Some people believed I had never aborted, that it was the same baby, that's how close together the pregnancies were. I felt a deep emotional hurt behind the decision to abort, but there was nothing I could do about it. Being pregnant again, I tried to stay clean. I went back to church, got into prayer lines, prayed and read my bible. For a while things seemed to be going well. In order to have a healthy baby, I had to stay clean. To avoid people who'd come by to tempt me into partying, I moved into my mother's house with my son and daughter.

With my two prior pregnancies, I never smoked or drank; I took prenatal classes and went the whole nine yards to insure my baby would be born healthy. I would go home from time to time to spend some romantic evenings with my children's father. Since he was such a butt head to me when I was carrying my son, I made an effort to spend quality time with him this time around. During one of our romantic evenings, I sent him out to get steak and shake for me and the kids. Hours went by no steak and shake; I'm getting real pissed off so I fixed the children something to eat and sent them to bed. Something told me to go down stairs; there I found that 'nut' smoking crack. If that wasn't bad enough, he had the nerve to offer me his pregnant baby mama some crack. Who does that? I'm pissed and weak in spirit and my flesh hadn't had a hit in months

I slipped and I smoked. God help me I thought to myself, its real close for me to deliver my child. We smoked all night up into the morning. I didn't think that this one time would hurt the baby any, besides I had over a month before I deliver, the crack would be out of my system by then. Who would know that my worst nightmare would soon occur?

A local carpet store had a 'carp dumpster', were they dispose of unwanted carpet remnants. The floor in my apartment needed an update, so my family and I went carpet hunting. There was a carpet at the bottom of the dumpster that I wanted, but it was so far towards the bottom, I had to jump in the dumpster to grab a hold of it. At seven and a half months pregnant it wasn't an easy thing to do, but I pulled and tugged until I was able to retrieve the carpet "wooh". To install the new carpet, I had to move back all of the furniture in my home. My place was a wreck, so I decided to stay at my mother's house, while the carpet is put in the next day. While at my mother's, I had to go upstairs to the bathroom, man them steps were steep as heck. While climbing the stairs, I lost my balance and fell. To be honest I didn't hurt myself at first, I chuckled with embarrassment, and went to the bathroom, then on to bed. A few days went by and I told my mother that my baby who is normally active, wasn't moving like she normally would. My mother didn't want to take any chances and decided to drive me to the emergency room. It was November 18, 1992. The doctors hooked me up to a baby monitor and realized that my baby was not moving properly, so I had to see an Embryologist.

The specialist performed an Amniocentesis – a procedure during which a long needle in inserted into the abdomen to extract amniotic fluid from the embryo sack for testing. When the doctor pulled out the needle the first time, the syringe was empty, the doctor had to repeat the test. This time, when the doctors pulled out the needle, my baby's heart rate dropped, we were code blue. My God, my God help us! I kept repeating to myself. (God's hand Is All Over Me). As they rushed me to the operating room, I remember the nurse asking did you take any medicine, any drugs. I said no because I had not done any drugs at that time. So what the heck was going on? Why was this happening to me? All kinds of thoughts were rushing through my mind. Just the words code blue made me think I was going to die or my baby was dying. I even thought God was getting me for that abortion I had, that this is judgment and I'm dying! Thank you Lord for your grace, mercy, and love

The doctors performed an Emergency C Section, and my daughter was air-lifted by helicopter to a nearby town that specializes in premature babies. (Thank you Lord "God's hand Is All Over Me.") My daughter and I survived that horrible experience, she was born about four weeks premature. There were some haters, believe me, there were many who hadn't liked me from way back, who called the child abuse hotline. As my daughter and I were getting ready to be discharged, a nurse came in to tell me that my daughter would not be going home with me and would be placed in foster care. I immediately called my mother who was a license child care provider to take my baby in so I could figure out all this craziness that was going on in my life. I left the hospital, but my baby remained hospitalized because her heart and respiration were irregular. When she was released, she was sent home with a heart machine. Thank God my mother had taken CPR classes in order to run her daycare. I knew my daughter would be in good care in case she stopped breathing or went into cardiac distress.

My life took a 360° turn. During my pregnancy, I stopped drugs, all but that one time with my kids father that cost me a bunch. I intended to be a good mom. Raising my children by myself then to lose it all for a small trace of cocaine in my system threw me off. Now I'm back out smoking and drinking. Why? My baby did not come home with me, so I'm having some kind of emotional crisis. I've never experienced giving birth to a child and not being permitted to take my baby home, to bond, to smell baby magic or baby lotion on my newborn or early morning feeding. I breast fed my other children, so I would pump my breast and take it to the hospital when she was there. I prayed to God to spare my child's life, and if he did I would give her back to him. I will raise her up to know and seek his face and I did. I held a dedication ceremony for my daughter and son; they were about three years apart so I made it a double ceremony. "God's plan is always at work." I went through the next few years feeling guilty because my daughter was developing behind everyone in her age group – behind in walking, behind in talking. Living with the role I played in my daughter's developmental delay tore me apart. I truly believe it was the botch up job the Embryologist did with that needle, after he could not withdraw the amniotic fluid and stuck me twice. Now I guess I'll never know the truth because the cocaine was a factor as well. The Lord has forgiven me and I moved on from that. We eventually adjusted to my baby staying with my mother and besides, she is just down the street. Grandmothers have been raising their grandchildren before the beginning of time

My birthday came on November 20, 1993. My baby girl had her first birthday on November 18, 1993. We had dinner at my mother's house and I'm headed to a friend's house where they are throwing a big birthday party for me. It was definitely popping, there were so many people there. One guy in particular kept looking at me. I felt like he was stalking me, but hey I looked good and he liked what he saw. We began to talk and dance, as the night wore on, he asked me to go to his house. I asked one of my friends if it's cool to go with him alone, my friend was like, girl yeah, he cool. ("God's Hand Is All Over Me.") Leaving with him meant we didn't have to be around a whole lot of people and we could enjoy ourselves, so I said sure I'll go. We go back to his house and had drinks, smoked a little bit, played some cards, and I began to get bored. It is my birthday, I didn't want to spend it at his house all night, I wanted to go somewhere and kick it at a night club or something, so I said "let's go somewhere". He's like "let's go upstairs for awhile, I want sex". I'm like, "that's not what I came here for". He said, "I didn't bring you to my house to let you drink up my alcohol smoke my dope and not give me sex, we going upstairs."

Again, I refused and he slammed me to the floor. I got up to run to the door. There was a skeleton key in the door which was locked from the inside and he had the key. I started screaming, crying, and hollering. He snapped and begun to beat me almost unconscious. The beating was too much. I felt I would pass out if he hit me one more time, so I gave in and went upstairs with him, where he repeatedly raped me. When he was finally finished, he went to sleep. Thinking he was sound asleep, I tried to get up from the bed. The movement of my body on the mattress woke him, and he sat up and looked at me. I knew it was game over if I didn't do some quick thinking, so I had to use some psychology. If he was expecting me to be hysterical, I was the complete opposite. I acted like we were cool, even though that bastard just beat and raped me repeatedly. I asked him to please let me call my family and children, because it's now 10:00 in the morning and I know my children are freaking out. I made him believe I would come back to his house, if he let me go see about my kids - he actually thought I meant it. As soon as I left his house I walked down that street as fast as I could to the corner phone booth and called my mom and stepfather to come and pick me up. ("Thank you lord for keeping me safe, I love you Lord")

My mother was curious about what happened to me that evening. I eventually told her the entire story and she encouraged me to go to the police. I didn't go to the cops because I felt they would probably make it seem like it's my fault for going to his house. At the time of my assault, date rape didn't get a lot of exposure; many people couldn't understand how a date could be rape; but when a woman says no to sex that's what she means. No one has the right to take sex from anybody. Shortly after my incident in 1993, date rape started getting coverage in the press, and more women started reporting their cases. When the time came for me to fill a report, I felt ashamed of the whole ordeal. I believed my God would seek vengeance for me as he had always done. God's word is true and can't come back void - *Psalms 105:15 touch not my anointed and do my prophets no harm.* Even though I did drugs, I loved the Lord. I knew I had some kind of purpose, but I didn't know what it was. That man is in prison today for selling drugs right after he raped me.

An existence of smoking, drugs and alcohol was not what God created me for. Tired of my lifestyle, I was out one night until the wee hours of the morning, walking and talking to God, giving God Praise and seeking his deliverance to heal me and make me whole, to deliver me from the craziness that was in my life. Going in and out of rehab, staying clean for short periods of time only to go back out again and use, was hurting not only me but my entire family. I cried out to God, "I said lord why won't you deliver me? I know you're able and I believe with all my heart my faith is larger than a mustard seed! Why won't you help me?" The Lord spoke to me in a loud voice; it's not your time! Satan tried to make me doubt God, but I knew that God knows best, so I searched his word about timing and due season *Ecclesiastes 3:1* as well as my favorite *Habakkuk 2:3* and *Jeremiah 1:5 he is the Lord of my life and he's working it out and everything is working together for my good. Romans 8:28 -for them that love God and who are called according to his purpose.* Now I'm in Holy Ghost training, from God's Glory to God's Glory! I began to take charge of my destiny and God was supernaturally guiding my footsteps. I moved out of my mother's house in 1994 into a homeless shelter so I could be displaced and get away from the drug environment that was in my neighborhood, to a better part of town in nice apartments.

Part of taking charge is being able to take care of my family. I began to work again at a nearby factory trying like heck to stay clean for me and my children. It worked for a spell; I stayed clean for about seven months, strengthening my promise through attending church and being very active in the church. A new member with his wife and children started attending. The new member was a deacon in training. At that time I was in the church for about fifteen years. We began to fellowship and clean the church; one day he asked me if I wanted to try some drugs. Well it's been awhile like seven months or so. I believed I could use and go back to my job and it would be different, I wouldn't chase the crazy drug. Just the opposite happened. During one of our smoking sessions we ran out of crack. Needing a new supply, we drove fifty miles to another town where we could get more. After our purchase, instead of heading home, we stayed in that town for hours smoking up into the night - at the lake front, in the park and out in the country in pitch black corn fields. Here comes the question, "can I have some sex?" Wow not again right? ("God's hand Is All Over Me") Of course I said no, his response was "then you'll walk". I'm thinking, once again you have put yourself in this situation because of this crazy drug, when are you going to live the life God has called you to. "My misery is my ministry". Determined not to go that route with him, I said "dude, I guess I better be about my walk because I'm not having sex with you." I got out his car and began walking.

Walking through that dark corn field, scared out of my mind, I just knew I was going to die. The moon was shining real bright lighting my way, and I began praying "Lord if you get me out of this corn field I promise never ever to smoke dope again." Before I could finish, here was dude pulling up next to me telling me to get in. Believe me, I thought twice about it, but in my spirit I felt it was cool so I got into the car. On our way back, he pulled out his dope pipe and asked if I wanted some – the Lord was putting me to the test right away. Resolved to sticking to the promise I made in the corn field I said no I'm good. My refusal didn't stop him; he lit his pipe and kept on smoking like a nut while driving. The shelter had a curfew for its residents, which I broke by staying out all night. When we got back into town, I was kicked out of the shelter. I moved in with my mother and within one week, my children and I were accepted into a nice apartment complex. The children liked the area. My son the swimmer was thrilled that there's a swimming pool. I loved the fact that I could plant flowers.

Prophetess and daughters, stepdad and mother in Cotton Field.

Prophetess' Grandmother

Our landmark of the south – fishing spot.

Prophetess at 16 years, 1976

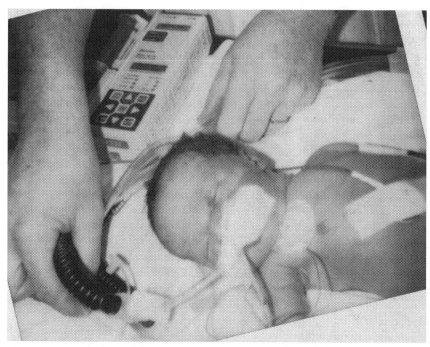

Birth of preemie baby 11-18-1992, ICU

Prophetess' three children and granddaughter
at their grandmother's funeral

The Beautiful Women in the Family

CHAPTER 2

Destiny Walk Begins. God's Spoken Word God's Hand Is All Over Me

I feel God's hand is all over me and his plan is always at work. Philippians 1:6 *God which has begun a good work in me shall perform it until the day of Jesus Christ.* Believing I was walking in my destiny on a purpose driven path, I decided to do prison outreach. I told one of my girl-friends to get me a number from her boyfriend, the next time she went to visit him in prison, and I'll pull someone out for a visit. Some inmates never receive visits after they go behind the wall, so if I could make someone's day I would; besides, being a clean, sober, drug free mom was beginning to get boring. While my children are in school, I'd get up early to go visit this guy my friend hooked me up with. After seeing each other on a daily basis we began to become close. In 1994, one year after we met we were officially dating. We were like closer than close; I went on family picnics and his family from Chicago would come and join us, my children would come out as well; we were like one big happy family. Being in the business since high school, an idea sparked – I no longer used drugs, but that didn't mean I couldn't sell it, especially in a place where you get more money than on the streets. Some people thought my boyfriend started that whole selling thing because he was the convict, not so; he was just the one who got caught. You'd think I would've learned my lessons behind all the trouble I've been in, but no, I'm penitentiary hustling. I know right?

My boyfriend and I had a good thing going, I would bring the crack and weed into the joint and my boyfriend would take it back to the population. We had a few guards who turned their heads as we took care of our business. It was hard to sit properly with the drugs stuck inside me, but as the money started coming in, that became less and less of a problem. With the extremes I had to go through to get the drugs into the facility, I didn't want to think about what my guy had to do to get it back to the population. As a matter of fact, I didn't want to go there, so I blocked it out of my mind. Believe it or not, leaving my apartment and going to the penitentiary was like going to another type of party. In 1994, the penitentiary was the place to be. We were having sex and smoking weed in the yard, it was cool like that, until one night I had a vision, "thank you Lord". ("God's hand Is All Over Me"). In my vision I saw myself taking the drugs in like always. When the time came for the Correction Officer to call me back for my visit, they began acting strange, looking and pointing, on the phone more than normal.

In my vision, they already had my boyfriend on lockdown and called me back to strip search me. I saw myself been arrested for possession with intent to deliver within a federal penitentiary. The next day I told my boyfriend of the vision and that I was done with hustling. The idea to sell was mine in the first place; he was cool with my decision. On my way home in the taxi I saw the local police pull up at the penitentiary. Could it be they were headed there to arrest me? I'll never know; what I do know is God sent me a warning vision which I obeyed. I never took drugs to the joint again. As our visit ended that day and I stood waiting for my taxi, I felt relieved that we were finished. However, through my little scheme I was now gang related and had served known killers from the east coast to the west. Chicago was family based; there were people from all walks of life who were incarcerated because of one bad choice. ("God's hand Is All Over Me") Thank you Jesus!

In 1997, things began to change in the penitentiary; a lot of women tried to bring drugs in and several got busted. That put the entire penitentiary on lock down. Random searches were performed. To avoid the drama, I started staying home more and just talking to my guy over the phone. We had been together for a while and it wasn't like he was going anywhere, he was locked up. When all the smoke finally cleared and it was safe to return to the penitentiary, I decided to stay home with my children. My oldest daughter became thuggish, hanging out with GO'S, smoking weed and drinking. I found out she was drinking when liquor went missing. I use to keep hard alcohol in the bottom of the cabinet, one night I came in from a date and we were all going to meet up for drinks because the clubs were closed. I went home to pick up some alcohol for mix drinks, grabbed the Tangueray Gin, got back to the party, poured the alcohol in glasses, low and behold it was water. Come to find out, my daughter and her friends drank all my gin and filled the bottles up with water. My 16 year old daughter is drinking, and from the number of water filled bottles in my alcohol cabinet, she was drinking a "bunch" as well as having sex. Later on that year my daughter became pregnant; I hate to say it but it was good, because she was headed to the penitentiary as well. "Gods plan is always at work".

My daughter was getting in trouble for home invasion. One evening I was sitting at home chilling with a guy friend and happened to look out the patio door, when I saw a detective walking my child down the sidewalk. Her pregnancy slowed her down a lot. I wasn't happy with her choice of baby daddy; she was pregnant by some white guy. I'm just keeping it real, that's how I felt back then before the Holy Spirit dealt with me about color. I've been a victim of racism; now I love God's people of all flavors. My daughter did a full 360 turn and prepared for her baby's arrival. Becoming a first time grandma in my case nana, I was too young to be called grandma, required that I made changes in my life also. My grand-baby wasn't due until early March, but she kept trying to come all of January and February as well. The doctor had to eventually give my daughter some kind of pills to keep her from going into labor. I began to seek the lord more and more.

Feeling God's power working in our lives brought me into a closer relationship with my lord. My family has this special calling; it started with a great great grandfather who stood in the gaps for his family decades ago. My family has a lot of ministers, missionary, Evangelist, etc. Some of us heard God's call and came forth; others like me came by way of drugs and alcohol. We had a powerful granddaddy who interceded on our behalf by the power of the holy ghost and god's promise that he would save him and his seed; *Psalms 28:8-9*. My first grandchild is under Satan's attack. I know she will one day become a massive weapon in God's kingdom when she joins the body of Christ and tear Satan's dark "kingdom down". The baby's due date isn't for another two months; I began to intercede on behalf of my daughter and grandchild. God is faithful; my daughter gave birth on March 3, 1998. Thank you Jesus! In 1998 a string of events started happening, it was like Satan picked my family's number and raised war against us. ("Gods Hand Is All Over Me")

A young white woman moved in upstairs from us. We've lived in the complex for about four years, so we have seen many people move in and out. There was something different about this young woman. I got an eerie feeling, my holy ghost warning me of her spirit. When I wasn't home, I had no clue what my children were up to. I later learned they would go upstairs and hang out with this woman; my daughter somehow managed to babysit for her little girl without my knowledge. My children knew when I left and when I would return, that's how stable my life had become. I was a grandmother who was falling deeply in love with my boyfriend who was on lock down in prison. My children loved the fact that my boyfriend kept me grounded and focused, they really liked him.

In December of 1998 I became a victim of conspiracy in that complex at the hands of that young woman who moved in upstairs; she started telling lies about my children and me. I didn't know her, I later learned that she had a very bad addiction to crystal meth and frequently hallucinated or just acted strange. Meth is one drug I hadn't tried "yet", but if it's anything like crack I don't think I would, it took what it felt like a lifetime to kick that crack addiction so I wasn't about to invite that monster in my life. This young woman's addiction to meth was so bad, she told the manager of our complex that I chased her up the stairs like I was trying to harm her. That episode never happened. I received information that the young woman and the apartment complex manager became real good friends; rumor had it that they were drug buddies. That bit of information did not seem factual – I've lived in the drug world, sold and done drugs with doctors and lawyers; drugs don't discriminate.

The Apartment Manager's behavior changed towards my family and me that year. At one time the manager and I were cool; we exchanged Christmas presents the year before, when she drew my name. Her sudden antagonistic behavior towards me was shocking. It was like a conspiracy, other white tenants in my building began spying on us and calling the police about various things all of it was just crazy. That year I got really scared, my family was the only black family in that building on that side of the complex; I feared for our safety, especially after I learned that the management was entering my apartment when we weren't home. My white neighbor friend, who lived next door, said she saw them and assumed I knew they were going in. I wasn't aware that a manager or landlord could enter a person's unit without permission, especially if nothing needed to be repaired. If I'm not mistaken, they are supposed to contact you for permission to enter. That year, maintenance or management kept entering my apartment as well as calling the police. In May 1999, I was arrested five times from false reports. The police department which consisted of all white officers allowed this type of harassment.

The harassment and false arrests continued, leading me with no alternative than to file discrimination charges against the apartment complex and the police department. I hired and fired two of the scariest, sell out lawyers in the Midwest. My family lost thousands of dollars in fees that we paid to those lawyers who did absolutely nothing. It was evident that I had to take matters into my own hand to represent myself in court. First I had to learn the procedures for filing documents and what type of documents I needed to file. I checked out law books from the local library, and began my law education. I filed motions for continuance, which the judge signed, that bought me time to obtain a good lawyer. In addition to harassment and discrimination, I was facing criminal charges of assault on a police officer and resisting arrest. My God I thank you for keeping me safe.

Those arrests were scary and very racial. There was one arrest that was so racist I can still hardly believe that it happened. One evening my next door neighbor and me were sitting outside when officers came around back to my patio and said Ms. Nicholson, we have a crime stopper report of loud music. Although I was surprised at the allegations I was very cooperative. I was home alone, my kids were at my mother's house; my neighbor and I were sitting outside quietly having a conversation. I told the officer I would allow him to arrest me and asked him to excuse me for a minute, so I can let my mother and children know my whereabouts. Normally, if I was going out I wouldn't call my mother's house, but I felt scared that if I left with this officer I wasn't coming back alive. While I was in my apartment placing the call to my mother, the officer came in behind me and locked the patio door; I totally freaked out. When the officer came after me I grabbed for my phone, and started beating him with the next thing I could get my hands on which was an umbrella. When he grabbed his walkie-talkie to call for backup, I started beating him with that.

Thank you Lord for sending angels to take charge of the situation. *Psalms 91:11 "I give you lord all of my love and praise".* Thank you Jesus, you are my hero. The officer brought out his mace and tried to mace me but mace himself. The mace got in his eyes and he couldn't see. I took advantage of the opportunity and ran out the front door to my next door neighbor apartment, my only white friend in my building, because I needed someone to witness this craziness. It was like some horror movie on television; she opened the door to let me and the officer was right behind me. He entered her apartment and I grabbed her broom and started to beat him with that! My God! Well he finally had backup, some more of his racist buddies came and I was arrested. That was alright because now someone else knew about it and they had to do it right; I was alive to tell my side. I believe if I had never ran next door to my neighbors that officer would've killed me and say that the gun accidently went off. ("God's hand Is All Over Me.")

Finally my time in court came. Our town's population is predominantly white, making my chance of getting a fair trial slim to none. ("God is a lawyer in the courtroom!) Although I was arrested for disorderly conduct and aggravated assault of a police officer, the judge gave me a fair sentence. He allowed me to keep my $3,000.00 bond to raise my son and ordered me to get counseling with my church or any mental facility of my choice. That was nobody but God. I did what the judge told me to do - I went to every church meeting I could; I had to hear a word from God, I had to be with fellow believers, I had to be in a setting with a Christian lifestyle because the devil tried to kill me! Thank God for God's people who believed me and how this bizarre thing could've happened.

It didn't stop there. The whites in the complex wanted me gone and at this point I was pretty glad about the Judge's decision. The calls to the police continued, however, the officers thought twice about coming to my apartment on stupid complaints, which made the other tenants furious. Information is power; I now knew the laws which protect me as a black American and did not hesitate to act when my rights were violated. The number of times I was arrested was grounds for eviction, but I wasn't leaving without a fight.

Having a place to live wasn't a problem; my mother owned four houses and I still had the one she bought for me and my children. Moving into that complex in 1994 was my way of having a better life, to get away from the influences that fed my drug addiction. The harassment and discrimination really pissed me off. Had the apartment management and tenants messed with me when I was out there robbing and heisting things out of stores on drugs, a menace to society, I could understand. Now that I'm clean and sober trying to live right to give my children stability, they want to destroy me? "Not," the fight is on! Bless God! I'm furious each time I remember what happened. Who did those people think they were? Black Americans are also Americans; we have rights as anyone does.

Unfair housing practices and discrimination is a federal offense; therefore, I took my complaints to the federal courts and the department of fair housing, charging my accusers of racial discrimination. The police department also had to be held accountable; I initiated charges for excessive force against the police department. My lawyer was able to stop the eviction pursuant to a stipulation the Judge approved, which specified that if calls or complaints were made against me within six months, the case would return to calendar, and a possible eviction would be enforced.

The six month period was reasonable; the charges from my white accusers were bogus. My family and I stayed away from that racist complex as much as possible, and when we were home my children and I were always on alert. When I went to work, other black residents in the complex looked out for my son; when I came home we were on lockdown. My son gained a lot of weight during that time; I wouldn't let him go outside, too scared for his safety. My concern was justified, those people were evil and wanted us gone by any means necessary.

Towards the end of the six months period I decided that I didn't want to live or raise my children where we are not wanted, loved or cared about. The month before our court date we began packing up our things, getting ready to move out. Living in that complex for those six months was a matter of principle; we're finishing what they started. Doing the six months probation would be a breeze, but fear will cause you to do strange things. Afraid that I was going to make my six month probation incident free, on the Friday before our Monday court appearance, the crooked racist manager of that complex sent me a letter stating she would be over that Monday for her yearly inspection.

I thought wow, why? We will be in court on that Monday and I'm moving out so why would she come over to inspect the unit. Everything we had was in boxes, what was she going to inspect? ("God's hand Is All Over Me") I wrote a response to her notice that an inspection wouldn't be necessary, that our court date was also Monday and to wait until afterwards. The woman writes me back, had it hand delivered and said no, she wasn't going to wait and would be over with the police at the date and time.

"Well it's on now." That Monday as I was getting ready for court I was in the shower and there was a knock at the door. My daughter opened the bathroom door and said them people are at the door. Before she could let them in, the police and the apartment manager were opening my door. I was butt naked stepping out of the shower; my daughter threw me a night shirt to quickly put on, and of course I freaked out, who wouldn't? I didn't know what these people were capable of; they have done some real strange things in the past. My first instinct was to grab for something to defend myself with. I grabbed a curtain rod out of the box nearest to me; the police man was getting ready to bash my head in. Oh God! I turned around and looked at my children's faces, thinking wow, this is 1999 and racism still exists. My kids were very upset, they said mom, why are they doing this? I couldn't answer because I'm not racist and I couldn't think like that, I couldn't hate anyone like that no matter what color. The policeman arrested me with nothing but that night shirt on, no underwear or shoes. Barefooted, he escorted me out through the lot so everybody could see that I was being arrested in a night shirt with no shoes on. I was so hurt, but I know "God is a healer and his plan is always at work".

My healing from that episode continues. If I don't forgive, how do I expect the Lord to forgive me for all the wrong I have done to people? The devil tried to take my mind at a time when I contemplated murder. The complex security guard played a role in the conspiracy to destroy me. He used to knock on my door and run. One night I caught him doing it; I ran out my door after him with a knife; as I caught him and was getting ready to slice his throat, I felt the Angel of God grab my hand. Thank you Jesus!

I didn't really want to hurt him, that's not my nature. I have hurt myself several times, over and over again, but someone else I couldn't, but they had pushed and pushed and pushed me so far, I felt my mind snap. If it wasn't for the lord on my side, I don't know where I would be – probably crazy, locked up in a psychiatric jail. ("God's hand Is All Over Me") That year I felt the power of God at work, goodness and mercy were at their post, the Holy Ghost was directing my foot steps and the angels were on assignment. Bless God! Believe me, I saw an angel right after that incident with that security guard; as I felt the presence grab my hand with the knife in it, I turned around and caught the very end of a white robe. Until this day, I'm not sure if it wasn't the hem of Jesus because I was definitely a woman with issues who desperately needed his touch. My situation depressed me, I was crying all the time, I felt despair. I'm giving God praise for allowing me to forgive my enemies.

My family and I finally moved away from that hell hole. The day I was moving, the whites in the complex were sitting out in their yards on lawn chairs in the rain. That's what you call hate. Who would sit outside in the rain watching somebody move? I was like some kind of side show in the circus; oh well I thought. I kept my head held high and continued to get my things the heck out of there! I received victory because no matter what was going on around me, I was spiritually blessed with God's Power, his love for me was manifesting itself in my life that year. *Acts 2:4 Blessing of the Holy Ghost with tongues of fire!* I went on the Potter's wheel *Jeremiah 18:2-4*, and I'm still on the wheel, bless God!

Becoming the woman of God that he called me out of the darkness to be, my enemies cannot curse what God has already blessed! Thank you Jesus!! I moved back to the neighborhood that I lived in where I was all strung out only to return clean and sober. Now that's God and I love him. I went on in June of 2000 and got married to yes my longtime prison lover, some called us Bonnie and Clyde; "Now" that's funny! He was transferred to another facility, and of course I followed him; he was moved three more times before his release. Life with him was real different; when he was about to be released, his parole officer came to my house to let me know what he expected from my husband after his release.

The parole officer said something that would change the course of our marriage for good; and once again another kick to my heart. This man who I have been with for seven years, who I thought was my soul mate and best friend had lied to me from the beginning as to why he was in prison. He told me he was serving time for murder by association. Not that murder is a better charge or anything, but in my book, it was better than sexual assault. My husband was incarcerated for sexual assault, also known to me as rape! I was shocked and disappointed. My husband never told me he was in for rape, and I couldn't let his parole officer know that my dumb butt of a husband failed to tell me the truth.

The parole officer went on to advise me that my husband will have to register as a sex offender and he can't be around children in a school district. I'm like wow, my mom is a childcare provider whose facility is right down the street from me, and I'm living in her house. What do I do? My husband who is a sex offender is going to be released and he can't come home to me.

The only other option I had was calling his aunt. I told her what the parole officer said – he can't come to my house, besides, I still had a case in Federal Court against the crooked police in this town. If they got wind of him living with me it could jeopardize my case, and they would rail road him back to prison. When he finally called me, I told him what the parole officer told me about him and asked him why he kept that charge from me. His excuse was, the girl who said he assaulted her, lied. Okay, females can lie about that, but I still wanted to know why after seven years of dating, marriage, being together from prison to prison, constantly supporting and standing by him through thick and thin, he kept the reason he went in a secret? I told him he can't come home to me, he has to go home to his mother. I had a pending case that I've been fighting for two years and it's close to being over. It wasn't about him; it was about me and my rights as a Black American woman with children, who is fighting with all she has to win.

My husband went home to his mother in Chicago. I later went to see him because it was our 1st anniversary. I continued to go every month to see him up until he started seeing some woman and got her pregnant. This woman wasn't the only one. I found out that he also had another pregnant woman on the west side of Chicago; both women gave birth to baby boys in the same month like two weeks apart. Wow, he was just nasty. He eventually violated parole and got locked up again.

God don't like ugly. A married man acting real brand new, and not only that he was married to God's anointed prophet; you better act like you know. I said that to say this – everybody who has ever said or done me wrong, God has allowed me to see them again. None of them were doing well, some were so tore up, I actually felt bad for them. God is faithful to his anointed prophets his word is true. My husband and I divorced in 2003 after he kept going in and out of jail. Thank you Jesus for your Glory! I could've been still married to this man, following him around from joint to joint, but there is a God. ("God's hand Is All Over Me.")

By the time my divorce was final, my life was headed in a new direction. I moved away from that small town to a town of 140,000 people of all different walks of life. This move was truly a blessing, people here didn't Judge you by the color of your skin, but as a person, who if given a chance to get to know, isn't so bad. I was glad I was here! Thank you Jesus! ("God hand is all over me")

My son was the only child I had with me at that time and he hated to leave his cousins and friends. Making the adjustment was a trying experience for him, but he knew his mother had suffered a mental breakdown and for her mental stability, he had to leave with her. I joined a really good church, got into their ministry leadership class, did really well in it. I was faithful to the call to ministry and had been strong in my faith until a new chain of events occurred. My step father passed on my birthday, November 20, 2003. I was out of town in Chicago when I received the call, and had to drive down for his funeral. On my way to his funeral I got pulled over for speeding, which was just great. After my move to my little house the bills started coming in. I called my son's father's family to see if I could get some kind of financial help because my son is getting ready to go to school and had no shoes, his shoes had holes in them. We had no refrigerator or stove and no money left, obviously no help either.

The church I had given my tithes and offering to couldn't help; to top it off, the utility company was getting ready to turn off my electricity. While I'm walking in faith it seems like once again all hell is breaking lose. I've suffered enough depression to last ten lifetimes, for one day I need peace. It's my birthday and I'm going to a nightclub and have a drink. Following the time I was raped on my special day, for a while I stopped celebrating my birthday. This birthday was going to be a good one because I was in a different city with new faces and a fresh new start. I wanted to forget all of my bills for just a little while. I took a long hot bath, tried to search my closet for some night club clothes because all I have now is church clothes. I've been back in church strong now for about three years. I had to rush out to the mall which is located down the street, found me some real sexy black pants with holes on the side of the leg and a nice red blouse to go with the outfit. While I'm getting dressed I'm starting to feel real strange, because I'm saved now, plus I was having flashbacks to when I was raped and beaten because of bad choices. Now I'm strong in church in ministry class, about to go out to the club because my emotions are taking over. I go out to a club and as I go to the bar to get a drink I'm carded, the bartender realizes it's my birthday – I get a free drink and they pin five dollars on me. The next thing I know, more and more people came up and pin money on me. What a way to celebrate my birthday!

I now have a good memory to replace that bad one; as I'm sitting by myself minding my business, an older gentleman in his 50s approached me for a dance. I'm not going to lie, the brother did look good, but he reminded me of an old time 70s pimp. He slipped me his pager number and asked if I wanted to go to another club? After all my bad choices in the past with men you have got to be kidding! I answered no I'm cool here, but I'll page you. ("God's hand Is All Over Me") We started dating a little bit at first; I would have him meet me at a local Wal-Mart or a movie rental place, I was not taking a chance of him being crazy like the rest of the men I had met in my life. This man was a trip though without luggage, I should have never started dating him. You see I didn't have any money and I needed help quick, fast, and in a hurry. We began to sleep together off and on, he already had a woman. What the heck was wrong with me that I felt the need to share a man? It's different when they cheat on you and you don't know about it, but when you know they have another woman and you're cool with that, there is definitely something wrong, and yes I had some serious issues.

God, you must really want me to be able to serve your people in every area of life because I am more than qualified. I how it feels to be molested, raped, on drugs as well as to struggle with addictions. How it is to be verbally abused, emotionally tore down by another human being, to be a victim of a hate crime as well as racism and now I know how to be one of the biggest "101" small time crack dealers within a 100 mile radius. My clients use to call me "The Doctor", a.k.a "G" for short. I struggled with selling a drug that I was a slave to; for me to sell it for a living was beyond my understanding. I had to do what I had to do, what I thought I had to do. There was no money coming and every bill is due like yesterday, so my old Mr. Pimp boyfriend hooked me up with the crack that I needed. He saw how good my sales were and decided to give me his dope to sell as well. I had to flip my own, selling his stuff too got real old – I put up with that because I didn't know where to get such large amounts at that time but that's soon to change. ("Gods hand is all over me") One time after I gave him all the money from the sell plus my re-up money, he took three days to call me; in the meantime, he was with his woman living high on the hog with the money I made. I needed either the money back or the dope and he is now M. I. A.

Time is money; I drove over to their house because he is not returning my calls. Dressed in all black with my hoodie over my head, I pulled up beside his truck, got out of my car, took my knife out and carved big gashes in the side of his truck. I figured I'm gonna get my money one way or another. I went back home and started making arrangements to get me some weight of my own. I called the little town where I just came from where all the drugs I ever needed was, I had smoked enough to know where to get and that's just what I did this time; I'm not using, I'm getting paid! Maybe I can make back some of the money I spent as an addict. It wasn't easy at first; I got ripped off a couple of times, then I had an idea. I stood out on the street and handed out tester packs to build up my clientele, it worked. It took about six months before I became well known; I had regular clients with great jobs. The one draw back was I lived 50 miles away from my clients, 100 miles round trip.

I commuted mostly on the weekends and it put a strain on my relationship with my Mr. Pimp boyfriend; yeah we stayed together after all that, but I didn't sell his dope anymore, he had to handle his own business. I made a lot of friends – even though they smoked crack they were people and I treated them like clients, I gave them good customer service and they made me their #1 dealer, WOW! The money I made was unbelievable, but on the other hand, things began getting strange and dangerous. I had a lady friend from Chicago III, a big time weight supplier, who had been traveling back and forth to that little town for years. Evidently, the police got wind of her arrival but we had no clue. It's Friday night and I was helping her serve the surrounding area drug dealers their weight and we had one more delivery. It so happened that I had some business of my own to take care of. "Hold up I gotta give the Lord praise!!" "THANK YOU JESUS! Once again you saved me from myself!" She had to make her own drop-off; as she was going to make that drop, the police were waiting in a dark driveway; when she pulled up, they opened her car door, threw her to the ground and put guns to her head. They had been expecting her all day. If I went instead of handling my own business, well let's just say I would be writing this book from prison. ("Gods hand is all over me") I went to visit her and also put money on her books, she is now seeking the face of God!! Who says God's plan isn't always at work "THANK YOU JESUS"

After that big drug bust, I continued to sell drugs for the next four years. There was one other time when I came close to another bust. As I rode by to pick up some weight, I saw the police standing by, while the water company turning off the water at the house where I was headed, then the police kicked down the door. I didn't stick around to watch what happened afterwards. ("Lord I thank you for keeping me safe!!")

The next few years didn't bring me any satisfaction. The money was good, I paid all my bills, took care of my son's bills, who is grown and living on his own, going to school doing really well, as well help my first born daughter pay some of her bills. I sold crack to take care of my family.

Feeling bored with my life, I began to party and drink with my clients. Although I didn't smoke crack, I began to snort coke and take pain pills, which quickly became an addiction. One night I was drinking, taking pain pills and snorting coke. I would trade crack for the pills so I wouldn't lose count of my money, and who really cares; I made so much money I would've never missed it, the turnover was so great. I remember my boyfriend wanted me to come home, we now live together and at this time we both agreed no staying out all night, so after consuming all those pills, coke and drink I had to drive fifty miles home ("Gods hand is all over me"!) I was good all the way home up to the sign that said I was near my town; at that moment I fell asleep! *He said he'd give angels charge over you Psalms 91:1.1* The angel of God took my car safely around a big bend and ramp on the highway that I know I should have died on; THANK YOU HOLY GHOST of being mindful of me in my fatal hour. Supernatural Powers took my car through head on traffic, lead my car around God only knows what kind of other dangers, because when I finally woke up from my drunken stupor, my car was on some old dusty country road near corn fields. I woke up and was amazed. My Lord loved me so much to save me when I couldn't save myself! I Love You Lord! That episode is one of many reasons that Jesus is my hero!

The Lord continued to show his favor. I was driving one day and there was a lot of snow and ice on the highway. I received a call about 500.00 dollars waiting on me to come and get on a drug sell, but I had to travel the 50 miles to get it, which was okay, that was my job and that was always the type of money I had waiting on me. The money was from one person, I was serving at least 20 people; I kept my circle of friends real tight. I didn't do new comers; these people had been with me since my crack dealership began in 2003. It's December 2005, holiday season, and they want to kick it. I'm on my way on the snowy icy road, when all of a sudden my car does a complete 360 in the middle of a busy highway. I was so blessed. Somehow I believe my Lord was warning me of trouble up ahead on the highway or maybe a possible bust; whatever it was, I have never been ignorant to the warning signs of the Lord. Remember he sent me a vision the time I was taking drugs to the penitentiary and that vision saved my life. I took the next exit right back home.

Prophetess – Easter Sunday, April 1999

Prophetess, Son and Granddaughter – Easter Sunday, April 1999

Church of God in Christ Loyalty Card

Prophetess, at the time, going out to visit husband in local prison

CHAPTER 3

Snatched into Purpose

I called my people and told them all money isn't good money, that I will not be coming, to find another dealer that lived there. I won't be mad because they had always been loyal, they never went outside of me to get their drugs, I was their girl G. The Lord has been so very faithful to me and my family. There was a time that my oldest daughter and I tried that crazy drug meth; to be honest, I HATED IT. It was a really stinky drug, it wasn't natural like the dope I was use to, it was made with everything under the kitchen sink, and so for me it was short lived. Besides, I was the dealer not a user anymore, and the buck stopped in my pocket. I wasn't about to make another dealer rich. My daughter started liking it so much that she became addicted; I refused to watch her die, wasn't about to let that happen, so I moved my daughter away from that crazy little town, the town that steals your hopes and dreams and moved her to the city.

The family curse stops now! As we were driving home as we often had done before, I began to share with my daughter that I was tired of dealing drugs and that the spirit of the living God is drawing me unto the kingdom and I have a work to do. My daughter has been with me while I've been in church as well as out of church and she knew I had always loved Jesus; as I began to share my plans with her, the Holy Ghost fell so strong on Me that I began to speak in uncontrollable tongues that I could not stop the spirit of God! He let me know that night on our way home to get my life in order it's time to go and represent The Kingdom of God. I immediately informed my clients that God has drawn me unto his Kingdom and that in 2007 I was making my way to heaven. They were not surprised, because they knew I was a very spiritual person and I never hid the way I felt about Jesus and they too have a deep love for Jesus. By them living in a place where the churches are judgmental and religion instead of a relationship with Jesus, my clients won't go to church. The bible states *"how can people hear unless there is a preacher"*, so in the meantime, Gods creation is perishing for lack of knowledge never really getting the chance to be truly introduced to our Lord and King and that's why I felt the need to write this book, so that we, the men and women of God, can get out there in the streets and get Gods lost people who have never been introduced to Jesus, because no one has brought him to them.

Matthew 9:37-38 the harvest is ready but the laborers are few. I pray the Lord send forth laborers into his harvest. I still witness to them as the Spirit of the Lord draws them closer to understand and know the truth about the victory that Jesus died for them that great and awesome day on the cross. They however are fighting all kinds of demons and they need strong Holy Ghost filled men and women to walk it out with them, because behind the drug demon there is the abuse of all kinds of demons, the molestation demon that led them to do drugs in the first place, the trauma of life that will drive them eventually to their death. In this last hour before Jesus returns, it is going to take men and women of God who are not afraid to put their devils on the run. God's Word in *Ephesians 6:12 we do not wrestle with flesh and blood, but against principalities against Rulers of darkness of this world against spiritual wickedness in high places.* Be aware!

In May 2007, I finally got job at a local store as a cashier, I love my new job. I even get a chance to talk and share my love for Jesus with my co-workers as well as customers who love to come through my lane, all is well in my life. My old Pimp boyfriend and I finally broke up, he left me that year for some older woman as it should be; he really was too old for me, and besides, God was supernaturally moving him out of my life anyway. I did not have the desire to be around him, we no longer shared the same interest, and I knew he could not go where I was going in God. Nothing or no one can stand in Gods way of my destiny and purpose, God won't allow it; so either you move it out the way or God will move it.

I was hurt by the breakup and the loss of another relationship. Thank the Lord for being with me through it all, and do or die, I'm here to stay with Jesus. He is my hero. No more looking for Jesus in all the wrong places or trying to find his love in way too many faces. Forgive me Lord, I know now you're the one who I adore, I know now that everything that happened in my life *worked together for my good Romans 8:28* and that *nothing shall separate me from the Love of Christ Romans 8:25* because I Know Who I Am, I know the Victory that Jesus overcame for me. Thank You Jesus! Through his healing power I can forgive my molester, I can forgive my abusers. I'm free from all my past hurts. THANK YOU JESUS!!! I'm working, living life the way it should be, free from drugs, delivered from people. I'm driven by God's Spoken Word.

On November 4, 2007, I got injured on my job. I was cashiering, it was the holiday season and people were shopping like no tomorrow and as always we were short of cashiers. Lines were backed up all the way to the clothes area; as I was scanning my items, my wrist began to sting real badly and I had to go report the incident to my shift manager, so we could put it on file in order for me to go to their company doctor. They sent me to take a drug test first and HEY! HEY! I passed it. The first test I can say I ever passed. There was a time in my life when weekly pee tests were ordered by rehab. I passed that one and it didn't surprise me, I'm living strong in the Lord and I know who I am. The store put me on light duty for awhile with a restriction of only working four hours cashiering and four hours in the clothing department. That arrangement worked for awhile up until one day I felt used. I had just finished my four hours cashiering because the company doctor said not to put too much strain on the wrist, so I'm off doing my job tagging clothes. My department manager comes and asked me to cashier. I told him my wrist was hurting and that I'm only suppose to cashier for four hours, doctors order. This inconsiderate manager told me to just go slow and I'll be fine. That's crazy, that's like me asking my children with bad colds to go outside and shovel snow, who does that? ("Gods Plan is always at work") The next day I went on and did like I was asked, I cashiered, going against company doctors. I contacted a lawyer because my right to properly heal from an injury was violated, and I needed my rights protected.

All of 2007 I was in so much pain but I refused to quit, for one I loved my job, it was honest and I know the Holy Spirit was with me training me to be a cashier. All my life I never worked as a cashier and I was good at it, that's how I know the spirit of God was with me. Some skills I had, I know came from him and only him. I went from company doctor to company doctor and they acted like they didn't know what was wrong or should I say, they didn't want to admit, I had gotten Carpal Tunnel Syndrome from processing their goods. It took the doctors until July of 2008 to admit it was their fault. In the meantime I'm working in so much pain, I had to take pain pills, which I had to struggle with taking, but what else was I to do, the pain was ridiculous.

I continued working that year. The company hadn't given me my workman's comp yet and I to go part time because I couldn't take the long hours anymore. Cutting back my hours at work was a difficult decision, but I'm yet trusting in God. I was tithing a percent of my work check and a portion of my child support check, so no matter what, I have money in God's bank. I had faith things will work out on my behalf; I'm saying to God – I have a mortgage and home insurance that needs to be paid, I really can't afford to work part time. The upstanding, honest life that I press through all the crap and drugs in my life to attain is now falling apart. ("Gods Plan is Always at work") I'm still not going back to sell drugs, I trust God! On Top of everything that's going on with my job, on Oct, 30, 2008 I received a call from my mother telling me that my baby cousin had been shot down on his college campus and is dead. MY GOD! MY GOD! He was only nineteen years old; too young to die.

For a few days before we were to leave to go to his funeral I kept feeling the spirit of God. I was about to drive my mother to Arkansas with Carpal Tunnel Syndrome. ("Gods hand is all over me") The Lord was with us as we traveled. My cousin's funeral was so big it was held at his school gym; people from all over the country sent e-mails, telegrams, flowers – countless expressions of love. Many of our children have been murdered just going to school. My cousin's death induced a lot of kids to give their lives to the Lord. I think of *Romans 8:28* again *that everything works out for our good*. My little cousin had given his life to the Lord a long time ago, so I'm comforted with the thought of seeing him again that day of rapture when we all will see Jesus. The dead in Christ shall rise first.

December 2008, they doctors decided to perform surgery on my right wrist. I will finally get some type of relief, a little too late. I'm three months behind on my mortgage, I'm about to lose my house. I'm expecting that because I legally paid my tithes and my offerings, I've stored up financial blessings. All I have to do is trust in God and if he doesn't keep my home it won't be kept! That December the surgery went well.

Having surgery on my right hand meant I would have limited movement. My mother came down to take care of me, to handle all of my needs while I recovered. I actually did well. She didn't have to wipe my butt as she thought; my mother was ready just in case though, she had her latex gloves, the whole nine yards. Mom stayed with me for two weeks, I was glad she was there; she got a chance to hang out with her daughter clean from drugs and sober, and that's a blessing right there, because once upon a time I'm sure she thought she would never witness her daughter clean and delivered from drugs. Thank You Jesus! ("I know it's you") On February 7, 2009 I had surgery on my left wrist; that surgery went well. As I got home there's a notice posted on my door for me to appear in court, I was being evicted from my home. Now that's great. After waiting two years, my surgeries have been completed but now it's too late to save my home; not to mention the courts gave me only seven days to move out.

God I need your help! I just had surgery, how and who am I going to find to help me move? Lord please raise me someone up to help me and sure enough he did. I went down to the local mission, there was always someone there looking to make money because they were homeless and you know what? Anyone can become homeless because that's what could've happened to me. I had nowhere to really go, I had to put my furniture in storage, even having to throw and give most of my most valuable things away, and move in with my daughter. As I put my things into storage, all along God was saying I will give you your hearts desires and increase your territory. To this day it has not manifested itself yet, but I'm trusting God's perfect timing. I trust God with my strength, my health and my prosperity! God's hand Is All Over Me, down this road to an incredible destiny, because I know his truth. Those are the very same words that the Holy Ghost placed in my heart.

I know my days ahead are a lot greater than those behind me. No matter what is going on in the natural world, I know that I am God's chosen and anointed for such a time as when this Soldier Prophetess will be called into full duty. This year I'm under the tutelage of a great Bishop Prophet who is an awesome man of God, who has spoken life and prophesy over me. Just as Jesus asks, *who does man say that I am?* Although Jesus was confirmed by God as his only begotten Son, man in the earth had knowledge of him as well, so confirmation by man went forth onto the earth. So when asked by man who do they say I am, Gwen King? They will say to you, that's Prophetess. Not only have I been confirmed by God but by man as well. Bless God! Who would have thought ME, Gwendolyn King, and all the hell I was in, would come forth as a strong, massive weapon in the Kingdom of God. Although God has allowed me to be stripped of my worldly things – house, car, clothes, like Job, my faith is strong, and I am steadfast in my belief in God, kicking the enemies butt, doing what God called me out of darkness to do.

That's my call to put the enemy on the run! Thank you Jesus! To go forth and tear down the kingdom of darkness. Every time you activate and workout God's word and go against the devil's plans, you've moved a little further in the kingdom of God. With me coming straight from a world of hurt and shame I had to pray to God for a clean heart and for him to renew in me the right spirit. Instantly God began to do some spiritual remodeling that had to take place. Whenever you remodel anything there first must come some tearing down. There are so many great changes in my life, my whole life has been a prophetic love story designed by the master builder. Everything that has happened in my life was not designed to kill me but to mold me, to shape me into the woman of God that I am today. God's spoken word went out before I was born and it has performed just what God sent it forth to do. *God's word will never come back void (Isaiah 55:11)* Gods spoken word kept driving at me, leading me to my purpose and destiny. Gods spoken word kept me from committing suicide, Gods spoken word said don't kill the racist he's not worth it (I GOT YOU), Gods spoken word spoke to my spirit and said, you won't always be an addict, you will overcome sexual molestation, rape as well as all your heartbreaks, YOU WILL FORGIVE!

God's spoken word speaks to my spirit saying: "My dear soldier Prophet, you overcame much. Your misery will become your Ministry." I call out in the name of Jesus! Every crack dealer, drug manufacturer, every crack, meth and heroin addict to repent! Accept Jesus as Lord and take your rightful place in the Kingdom of God! I call out in the name of Jesus! Every pimp and prostitute to repent and accept Jesus Christ as Lord and to take your rightful place in the Kingdom of God! I call out every murderer and rapist to repent and come unto Gods throne of mercy, grace and Love; receive the Lords forgiveness, accept him as Lord and take your rightful place in the Kingdom of God! I call out in the name of Jesus every broken abused heart and soul to come unto Jesus accept him as Lord over your life, let him mend the broken pieces and let our Lord that has begun a good work in you perform it until the day he comes for you. (Philippians 1:6) Come now! Come now! While you still can! The King of Glory is coming soon!!! Once you accept your calling you are then happy in all that you do. The Lord has opened so many great and awesome doors for me that I know no man can shut! Although life has tried to bring me many setbacks, God has set me up for his blessings! And through it all he has taken me to another higher dimension in him. There is nothing or no one in this world that God cannot restore, revive or return back to his original purpose. I know I'm just where God wants me to be, though my vision, hopes and dreams are for an appointed time, they shall surely come I just have to be patient, I have to wait on the Lord! I MUST HAVE A HABAKKUK STORY!

Community mourns victim of school shooting

RACHEL DENTON FREEZE
Times-News Staff

Dermott teachers and students are mourning the loss of a former student and classmate.

Chavares Block, a 2007 Dermott High School honor graduate, was one of two students killed at a shooting at the University of Central Arkansas Sunday night.

Block, 19, was in his sophomore year at UCA and studying to become an engineer.

"He was a model student," said Dermott High School Counselor Lottie Bunn. "He always put his academics first."

Block was an advanced honors student at Dermott and served as President of the Senior Class in 2007. The young man was involved in variety of school organizations while

Chavares Block

in high school including the Beta Club and the Ram football and track teams.

Teachers and administrators described Block as "respectful" and "well-mannered."

"He was an example of youth at its best," Bunn told the *Times-News*. "He was just a wonderful young man and we are going to miss him."

See School Shooting, Page 10

School Shooting

Continued from Page 1

Bunn said the school is providing counseling to students to help them deal with the loss.

"It feels like you've just been punched in the stomach," said Bunn. "Yesterday, teachers took the opportunity to let students just breathe."

The school is planning to memorialize Block by creating an internet blog where students can express their condolences and memories as well as a memory wall at the school honoring him. Dermott EAST lab students have also designed t-shirts honoring Block and organized a candlelight vigil at the downtown Dermott gazebo last night.

Block was the youngest of the three sons of Raymond and Martha Block of Dermott.

Conway police said there are four men in custody in connection with the college shooting. Police identified the suspects as Kawin Brockman of Conway, Kelsey Perry of Morrilton, Mario Toney of Little Rock, and Brandon Wade of Lake Village.

No statements have been made concerning a motive in the case, but authorities said none of the four suspects were students at the university.

Funeral arrangements for Block were not available at press time.

Prophetess, two best friends, 12-31-2004

Prophetess and her armor bearer

CHAPTER 4

Prophetess Prayers
Prophetess Official Documents
Birth Certificate
Unfair Arrest Record
Documented Signatures to Support Conspiracy Claim
Mental Progress Report
Church Letter of Acceptance

The Davidson Family Tree

Octavia Davidson (Kilpatrick)

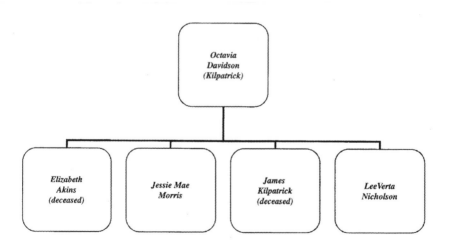

Octavia Davidson's
(Kilpatrick) Family Tree

Octavia
Davidson
(Kilpatrick)

Elizabeth
Akins
(deceased)

Jessie Mae
Morris

James
Kilpatrick
(deceased)

LeeVerta
Nicholson

Elizabeth Akins' Family Tree

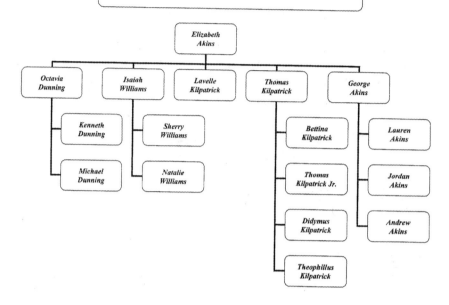

Elizabeth Akins

- Octavia Dunning
  - Kenneth Dunning
  - Michael Dunning
- Isaiah Williams
  - Sherry Williams
  - Natalie Williams
- Lavelle Kilpatrick
- Thomas Kilpatrick
  - Bettina Kilpatrick
  - Thomas Kilpatrick Jr.
  - Didymus Kilpatrick
  - Theophillus Kilpatrick
- George Akins
  - Lauren Akins
  - Jordan Akins
  - Andrew Akins

Elizabeth Akins' Family Tree
(continued)

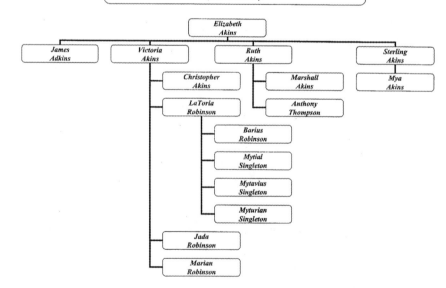

Elizabeth Akins

- James Adkins
- Victoria Akins
  - Christopher Akins
  - LaToria Robinson
    - Barius Robinson
    - Mytial Singleton
    - Mytavius Singleton
    - Myturian Singleton
  - Jada Robinson
  - Marian Robinson
- Ruth Akins
  - Marshall Akins
  - Anthony Thompson
- Sterling Akins
  - Mya Akins

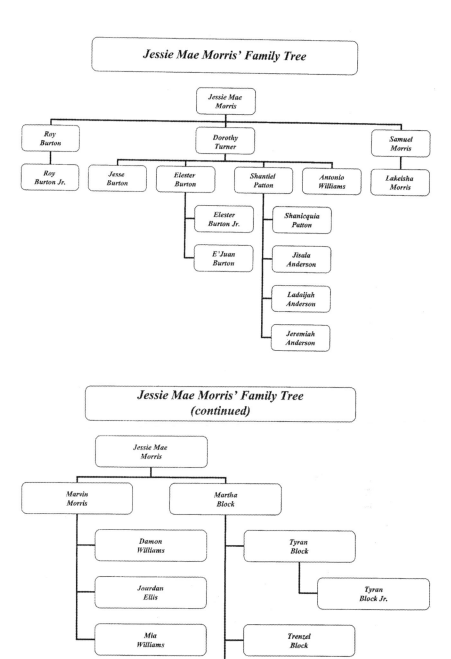

Jessie Mae Morris' Family Tree

Jessie Mae Morris

Roy Burton

Roy Burton Jr.

Dorothy Turner

Jesse Burton

Elester Burton

Elester Burton Jr.

E'Juan Burton

Shantiel Patton

Shanicquia Patton

Jisala Anderson

Ladaijah Anderson

Jeremiah Anderson

Antonio Williams

Samuel Morris

Lakeisha Morris

Jessie Mae Morris' Family Tree (continued)

Jessie Mae Morris

Marvin Morris

Damon Williams

Jourdan Ellis

Mia Williams

Martha Block

Tyran Block

Tyran Block Jr.

Trenzel Block

Chavares Block

LeeVerta Nicholson's Family Tree

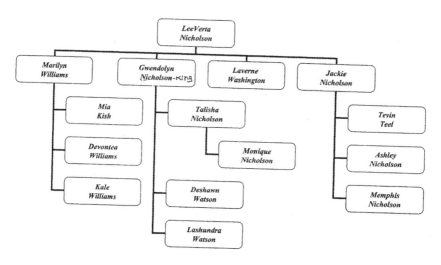

Registration District No. **14**

Primary Registration District No. **3018**

ARKANSAS STATE BOARD OF HEALTH
Bureau of Vital Statistics
CERTIFICATE OF LIVE BIRTH

'60 **032736**

1. PLACE OF BIRTH a. COUNTY *ASHLEY* DEC 19 1960	2. USUAL RESIDENCE OF MOTHER (Where does mother live?) a. STATE *ARKANSAS* b. COUNTY *AS*
b. CITY, TOWN, OR LOCATION *PARKDALE*	c. CITY, TOWN, OR LOCATION *PARKDALE*
c. NAME OF HOSPITAL OR INSTITUTION (If not in hospital, give street address) *Ro.# 254*	d. STREET ADDRESS *Ro# 254*
d. IS PLACE OF BIRTH INSIDE CITY LIMITS? YES ☑ NO ☐	e. IS RESIDENCE INSIDE CITY LIMITS? YES ☐ NO ☑	f. IS RESIDENCE ON A ... YES ☑

CHILD

3. NAME (Type or Print) First *Gwendolyn* Middle Last *Nicholson*

4. SEX *Female* | 5a. THIS BIRTH SINGLE ☑ TWIN ☐ TRIPLET ☐ | 5b. IF TWIN OR TRIPLET, WAS CHILD BORN 1st ☐ 2d ☐ 3d ☐ | 6. DATE OF BIRTH *Nov 20 1960*

FATHER

7. NAME First *Otis* Middle Last *Nicholson* | 8. COLOR OR RACE *Negro*

9. AGE (At time of this birth) *22* YEARS | 10. BIRTHPLACE (State or foreign country) *Alabama* | 11a. USUAL OCCUPATION *farmer* | 11b. KIND OF BUSINESS OR IND *tractor Dri*

MOTHER

12. MAIDEN NAME First *Leverta* Middle Last *Kitpatrick* | 13. COLOR OR RACE *Negro*

14. AGE (At time of this birth) *26* YEARS | 15. BIRTHPLACE (State or foreign country) *Arkansas* | 16. PREVIOUS DELIVERIES TO MOTHER (Do NOT include this bir

| a. How many OTHER children are now living? *0* | b. How many OTHER children were born alive but are now dead? *0* | c. How many fetal (fetuses born dead time after concept |

17. INFORMANT *Leverta Nicholson*

18. MOTHER'S MAILING ADDRESS *Ro.# 254 Parkdale Ark*

I hereby certify that this child was born alive on the date stated above. | 18a. SIGNATURE *Wilma Walker* | 18b. ATTENDANT AT BIRTH M.D. ☐ MIDWIFE ☐ OTHER ☑ (Specify)

18c. ADDRESS *Ro# 205 Parkdale Ark* | 18d. DATE SIGNED *Nov 29 1960*

19. DATE REC'D. BY LOCAL REG. *Dec 13 1960* | 20. REGISTRAR'S SIGNATURE *Katsie L. Oliver* | *12-13-60* BY *RLO*

THIS IS TO CERTIFY, That the above is a full, true and correct copy of the original certification which is on file in this office and of which I am legal custodian. IN TESTIMONY WHEREOF, witness my hand and seal of office at Little Rock, Arkansas.

June 23, 1961   State Registrar

Prayer of Thanks

Dear Heavenly Father, Lord I'm at your throne of mercy grace and love. Lord cleanse me with the redeeming blood of Jesus. Lord I thank you for giving me the strength to write this book! The courage to confront demons from my past! Lord, although it was hard to put everything you have done for me in this book, like the time when the hot antifreeze shot out the car onto my face, no burns, your grace is always sufficient! Your grace of protection covered me! Thank You Lord! Lord I also want to thank you and let them know how you showed up again when I got knocked in the head by a drunk with a 40oz of beer and how my head began to shoot blood and how you plugged it up to stop the bleeding. I knew it was you, and I know how your Shekinah Glory showed up and protected me once again from a heroin addict, who beat me in the head with a hammer and I walked away with only a black eye, letting people know you showed up and showed out. The ever present, all powerful, all knowing God that you are, you knew I'd stand up and tell it just like it was, no Buddha or Muhammad, but my God. The One, True, Living God of the Bible.

Lord there is so much you have done for me to show me just how much you loved me; I can't begin to tell it all! I love you.

Prophetess Prayer

I call out in the name of Jesus, every spirit that is bound by lack of knowledge that thirsts for the Lord. I send forth the Holy Spirit in the Name of Jesus to raise up pastors and strong Holy Spirit Ministers to serve God's lost children and bring them into God's Kingdom. I bind every hindering spirit that comes against the seed of freedom; this seed shall go forth in the name of Jesus to free God's people! I come against all spirits of darkness to let God's people GO Now! In the name of Jesus! Right Now! Right Now! Lord we give you all the praise and Glory for the victory! Amen! Amen!

The spirit of the Lord is upon me. I speak to the spirit of all that are being supernaturally drawn by the spirit of God, *Joel 2:28,* to an instant quantum leap! For the King of Glory shall come! The only begotten son of God is to come.

It's almost as if you would close your eyes and reach up, you can feel him stretching his hand to snatch you, his people up! God Bless! Thank you Jesus! The spirit of the Lord says, tell my people to hit this extra strength 21st Century Devil from the kingdom of darkness, hit him with *Galatians 5:22, fruit of the spirit is love, joy, peace, longsuffering, gentleness, goodness, faith, meekness, and* temperance, doing everything in your power to withstand these things. *Put o your whole armor of God Ephesians 6:13-21 with truth and righteousness!* With peace the shield of faith! The helmet of Jesus salvation! The sword and spirit of God's Almighty working word! Bless God! Give him Glory! Right there!

The Lord has warned us through his holy word on what to expect and has equipped us in this hour with ammunition to defeat the kingdom of darkness, just in case the devil didn't read the end of God's word. We the children of God win!!! Give the King Glory his praises!! Hold on God's people, fight with all you have, fight with the power of the Holy Spirit. I promise you, you will win every battle that you face in this supernatural war that has been set before you.

Bless you!!
People of God I Love You,
Prophetess Gwendolyn King
September 28, 2009, The Day of Atonement.

Prophetess Final Words

From the pit to the palace (Genesis 37:27)

There are times in this destiny walk when I felt like Jacob and Joseph, chosen and blessed by God with purpose and promise, on my way to the blessing by way of a dark, dry, lonely painful pit, and although I'm in this place I prayed Lord! I'm not letting go until you bless me! (Genesis 32:24) Lord! I'm holding on to your word! I'm holding on to this holy faith! I'm holding on to your lifestyle, to your character! Even while I'm in this place, I'm not letting you go Lord. Until you dig me out into your palace.

The Lord has sustained me and my family through all those hard times, the painful times, the times of lack and not enough. Like the women in 1ˢᵗ Kings 17:16, as her meal and oil never ran out, my family and I are blessed the same.

The Lord has hidden me in dry places; he took me through the process, from being Sister Gwen in the church to prophetess Gwendolyn, a prophet to the nations. He purposely raised me up as one of his champion heavy weight contenders of this Holy Faith, for the special event of gathering the harvest, Mathew 9:37. Not having any fancy degrees or an eloquent speech that even qualifies me, only the Holy Spirit of God has armed me with his dynamite anointing power! To stand firm against any devil or demon!

God's Word (Hebrews 4:12)

God's Word
(For the word of God is quick and powerful, and sharper than
any two-edged sword, piercing even to the dividing asunder of
soul and spirit, and of the joints and marrow, and is a discerner
of the thoughts and intents of the heart. Hebrews 4:12)

Gotta believe in the living God,
Every word he spoke over me
My faith is larger than a mustard seed.
Jesus victory lives deep inside of me,
(Because I know the truth!)

Let Gods word set your free,
Look for the truth and you will see
That God's word will set you free.

My life is riding on him,
He has created everything that I am,
My health, my strength, my prosperity.
God's hand Is All Over Me,
Down this road to incredible destiny
(Bless the lord!)

Let Gods word set you free,
Look for the truth and you will see,
That Gods word will set you free.

Everything I hoped I would be,
The dreams for my life I thought I could never achieve.
But I keep holding on,
Pressing through all of life's storms,
Living out Gods purpose,
From the day I was born
(Gods Purpose).

The devil comes to deceive and destroy,
The Lord has rebuked you!! I rebuke you!
And now my life has this incredible joy!
(Bless the Lord!)

Let God's word set you free,
Look for the truth and you will see,
That God's word will set you free.

God's word!
(Philippians 4:13)
That you can do all things through Christ which strengthens you!

God's word!
(1 Peter 2:9)
That you are of a Royal Priesthood, a chosen generation, Blessed by God.

God's word!
(Habakkuk 2:3)
That your vision, hopes and dreams are for an appointed time and
though it tarry (wait for it) For it shall surely come (If you faint not!)

God's word!
Revelation 1:7
That Jesus is coming on clouds; that every eye shall see
and "every knee shall bow' (Philippians 2:10-11)

God's word!
Psalms 24:8
For behold you will see the King of Glory!
Who is this King of Glory? He is our Lord,
mighty in battle and He shall come in!

Let God's word set you free,
Look for the truth and you will see.
That God's word will set you free.

Written by:
Prophetess Gwendolyn King
June 28, 2009
Genre: God's Inspirational Gospel (Good news)
Inspired for such a time as this

Jesus Put His Life on It

My life is built on nothing less,
But Jesus blood and his faithfulness,
Heaven and earth we will possess,
When we stand and believe in Gods Promises,
Jesus is the rock that you can rely on,
All other ground is sinking sand.
Jesus is the rock which you can stand on for your life,
(for your life)

Jesus put his life on it,
He put his life on it,
Jesus put his life on it.

He said he'd never leave your or forsake you,
As life's trials and tribulations come and they will go,
But you let the words of the Lord burn deep in your soul,
You take a Hallelujah praise, Satan must obey.

Jesus put his life on it,
He put his life on it,
Jesus put his life on it.
(Fade out music)

Jesus that always was (Hallelujah)
Came to earth just to save us,
You put your life in his hands and
He will help you with his plan for your life
(for your life)

Jesus put his life on it,
He put his life on it,
Jesus put his life on it.
(Fade out music)

Heaven and earth will pass away,
But his merciful love is here to stay.
The day that he shed his blood,
Was the way he showered perfect love.
(for your life)

Jesus put his life on it,
He put his life on it,
Jesus put his life on it.
(Fade out music)

Written By:
Prophetess Gwendolyn King
May 5, 2008
Genre: God's Inspirational Gospel (Good News)
Inspired for such a time as this

I Can Hear the Lord Say

When the storms of life are raging, and the things of this ole world have your mind in a swirl, I can hear the lord say, stay strong, I'm leading the way! When your mountains and your valleys everyday are staring you in your face, you're walking around with a frown because your life has been turned upside down.

I can hear the lord say, trust me never doubt. I'm your Lord and Savior, I love you, I died for you! I'll bring you out! I can hear the Lord say! I can hear the Lord say! I can hear the Lord say! I can! I can! I can hear the Lord say! Foreclosure, divorce, bankruptcy, kids acting up! I can hear the Lord say! Don't give up and don't you fear! Your King of Glory is standing right here! I can hear the Lord say! Greater is he that is in me than he that is in the world! I can hear the Lord say! I can do all things through Christ who strengthens me!

I can hear the Lord say! All things work together for good, for those who love the Lord. I can hear the Lord say! I can, I can hear the Lord say!

Written By: Prophetess Gwendolyn King
October 20, 2009
Genre: God's Inspirational Gospel (Good News)
Inspired for such a time as this.

I Love You Lord

If I never had any struggles or trials how could you show – that you're the only true living God. Lord you raised me, you saved me, you picked me up and turned me around, you placed my feet on solid ground; put a new song and dance in my heart, you knew my destiny and purpose right from the start, you knew just what I've been going through.

I Love you Lord, I Love you Lord, I Love you Lord, I Love you Lord, each and every day, in my heart you'll always stay. (Hallelujah)

Lord I looked for you in all the wrong places, tried to find your love in too many faces. Forgive me Lord I know now, that you're the one that I adore. And I'm knock, knock, knocking on heaven's door. I'm knock, knock, knocking on heaven's door. (Bless you Jesus)

Holy spirit you are the one, sent to comfort by God's only begotten Son (Bless you Holy Spirit). Now I know what true love feels like, I wanna thank you for keeping me through all of my crying and sleepless nights. Bless you Holy Spirit for the work you've done inside of me; you came into my life and set my spirit free. (Hey, Hey, Hey)

I Love you Lord, I Love you Lord, I Love you Lord, I Love you Lord, each and every day in my heart you'll always stay.

(A word from Prophetess Gwendolyn King) Soldiers of our Lord King, we must continue to contend for our Faith like never before; we are in position and conditioned with the Holy Spirit to win. In the name of Jesus! Amen, Amen!

Written By: Prophetess Gwendolyn King
Genre: Gods Inspirational Gospel (Good News)
Inspired for such a time as this

I just wanted to let the people know
That whatever you need Gods got it!
He is the same God of the bible yesterday

Today and forever more
And the Lord still Loves, Saves, delivers!!
And most of all his mercies are new everyday!
I Thank you God for giving us you're only begotten
Son to die for us that we may live forever.
I Love You.

Respectfully your servant
Prophetess Gwendolyn King

A Prophetic Word to the Believers
(God saved the best for last)

The Lord saved a special remnant for last, they are
The Kingdom of God's Champion fighters, they are the least likely
Who became the most likely
The true contenders of the Christian Faith
For people who have a Lazarus experience (St. John 11:1-4)
Who have prayed and prayed to the Lord for help and deliverance
Only to feel like their time hadn't come yet.

It's not that the Lord doesn't love you because he does
But he waits so the world will know that it was she and him alone
That has delivered and bought you out for the Glory of God (St. John
11:40) With the world's vast need to extra strength,
Everything from pain relievers to extra strength laundry soap
There is a people that God is using in this end time spirit war,
Who go looking for Satan's camp without fear!
For they know who they are,
And what God redeemed them out of the enemy's hand to do.
(Psalms 107:2) If the world and all its troubles couldn't break them
down, surely no devil or his demons will!!!
They are a people who read God's word
And know no matter what is going on around them, they will win!!
As we go forth now to prepare for our hero,
Our Lord King of Glory to return,
Remember God's people, we already won this war!
Keep your faith! Never doubt, Jesus is Lord!

The risen savior he loves!
He is bringing us out with A victorious shout!
As we watch and continue to pray, remember the words of the Lord
(St. John 14:27) Peace I leave with you, my peace I give unto you
Not as the world giveth, give I unto you
Let not your heart be troubled neither let it be afraid.
God's plan is always at work, hold on help is on the way!

Press your way just like the woman with the issue of blood, (Luke 8:43)

Prophetess Gwendolyn King prophesying
To the world of believers in Jesus
November 23, 2009

Prophetess Gwendolyn's gong lyrics
Song written by: Talisha Nicholson
Song Title: I want to thank you

I want to thank you for all that you've done for us. We know just where our blessings come from. Your word is the truth Hallelujah to you, without you what would I do.

I've spent so much time on a search to find certain things that weren't good for me, that brought me down crying on my knees. But one day I called on Jesus' name, it was the sweetest name that I've grown to know. He broke yokes and pulled down strongholds!

Your love for me is forever strong, without you in my life I would go down wrong.

Loving with stretched arms my Savior is near saying "Child don't you fear. Your heavenly Father is here, to guide you into a better life. You don't have to think twice, I'll never leave your side. It's the best decision of your life."

This time I'll be brand new, but if only you knew how many times I said those words. Now I know the world's way never works. Only he knew the tears I cried; now this lovely, worthy butterfly must take a chance and spread her wings, Gods love will make you do righteous things.

So I placed my heart under lock and key to take some time to take care of me. Still loving with stretched arms my Savior is near, he's right here! Whom shall I fear? The Holy Ghost is here guiding me through life. Never leaving my side always on time. This was the best decision of my life.

UNITED STATES DISTRICT COURT
CENTRAL DISTRICT OF ILLINOIS

NICHOLSON, WATSON CASE # 01-1199
V.
GALESBURG POLICE DEPARTMENT

DOCKET ENTRY_ TO GIVE THE COURTS A MORE DEFINTE STATEMANT

ON APRIL 29 1998 A SIGNED COMPLAINT BY OFFICER
BARRY D. HUFF# 82 TO ARREST MY MOTHER GWENDOLYN KING PLAINTIFF #
00-1353 FOR A DISORDERLY CONDUCT- RUDE AND OFFENSIVE
IN A SUPPOSINGLY VIOLATION OF A SECTION 15-110 CHAPTER 15
THE ARREST WAS NOT MADE UNTILL THE NEXT DAY BECAUSE MY
MOTHER WAS AT WORK.

ON THE NEXT DAY I BELIVE IT WAS ABOUT 1:30 IN THE AFTERNOON
A GOOD NEIGHBOR IN THE NEXT UNIT TOLD MY FAMILY THE POLICE
WAS HERE YESTERDAY WHICH WAS THE 29TH OF APRIL WHEN MY
MOTHER AND I LEARNI WE CALLED THE STATION TO ASK THEM THE
NATURE OF THEIR VISIT, ALL THEY SAID WAS WE NEED TO ARREST
GWENDOLYN NICHOLSON (KING) WHEN I ASKED THEM WHY THEY
SAID WE LL TELL YOU WHEN WE GET THERE I RELAYED THE MESSAGE
TO MY MOTHER GWENDOLYN KING AND AT THAT TIME MY MOTHER
THEN SAID TELL THEM TO COME BUT FIRST SHE NEEDS TO PHONE
HER JOB AND SHE DID JUST THAT AND THE POLICE CAME AND AT
THAT TIME STILL NOT KNOWING THE CHARGE , MY MOTHER AND I
KNEW IT MUST OF BEEN THE RACIST PEOPLE IN THE COMPLEX
CASE# PENDING NO 01-1911 KING V A&R KATZ SANDBURG VILLAGE
APT.

WHEN MY MOTHER AND I TRIED TO RECIVE THE SAME SERVICE AS
OBVIOUSLY THE WHITES HAD RECIVED WHEN THEY PLACED THE
FALSE CALLED WE WE WERE REFUSED I TALISHA NICHOLSON WITNESS
MY MOTHER BEING SEARCHED FOR DRUGS AND WAS ARRESTED NOT
KNOWING THE CHARGE AT THAT TIME AND SHE WAS DETAINED FOR
HOURS BEFORE THEY FINALLY TOLD HER THE NEIGHBORS SAID
YOU WERE BEING OFFENSIVE . I TALISHA NICHOLSON WITNESS
HOW THE POLICE NEVER ASKED US WHAT HAD HAPPENED IF ANYTHING (G.P.D)
REALLY DID HAPPENED OR NOT THEY ARREST HER ON WHAT THEY SAID (THEY)
VIOLATED OUR RIGHT TO BE TREATED EQUALLY (4TH AMENDMENT)
AND THE UNLAWFULLY SEARCHED HER PERSONS.
OF

pge 1 April 20th 98
pge 2 may 5th 98
pg 3 april 29 98 may 24
pge 4 Sept 23rd 1998

78

FILED

MAR 1 3 2001

JOHN M. WATERS, Clerk
U.S. DISTRICT COURT
CENTRAL DISTRICT OF ILLINOIS

United States District Court
Central District of Illinois
March 10, 2001

Case #1:00-CV-01353
Title: King vs. Galesburg Police Department
Docket Entry-Answer to the defendant motion
For a more definite Statement

CONFUSED ABOUT DATE BUT CLOSE

Answer- On or about May 1, 1998 I placed a call to the
Galesburg Police Department to report a lady harassing and
following my 8 yr old son around while I was at work and my son
was trying to play on the playground with other kids at the sanburg
village apartments play area. Officer Damon Shay answerd the
dispatchers call to investigate my complaint upon his arrival I
stated what my son had reported and his concerns and because my
son was so afraid it took him a few days before he even told me.
Officer Shay then went up stairs to the 2nd floor of the building my
family and I lived in to the lady in question after a few short
minutes the lady and Officer Shay both came back downstairs
laughing as they bypassed my son and I, so we proceeded to go to
the 3rd building down from my building of 676 Home Blvd. I
began to follow behind them, telling my son to go to a close good
neighbor, while I go to see about my complaint and to see if it was
being properly looked into. I then notice Officer Kip Canfield
came on the scene in plain clothing (no uniform) and a few other
unknown officers. The lady in question, officer Shay along with
Kip Canfeild all began to walk to the office of Sandburg Villiage
Apts, apt#666 Home blvd Galesburg Illinois 61401 , and they
closed the door in my face, Now as concerned mother about her
sons well-being and safety, while I'm working, I decide to take a
seat and wait for some kind of justice as I sat by myself outside the
office I began to feel like they weren't taking my complaint or my
sons concerns seriously. As all the parties came out I asked about
my complaint and by the looks they gave me after I asked my

Exhibit 1

79

question,it frightened me so I just went out of the building upon leaving the building I ran into a lady who could witness to them to what happened and the officers ignored us as though it wasn't important. A statement like we don't have time to talk to you or your witness and they all proceed to walk away from us.Right then and there I realized that my constitutional right to be protected and treated equally had just been violated. Leaving my 8yr old son and I feeling less than human beings. My witness will testify under oath upon request. See King vs.A&R Katz 1:00-cv-01331

On or about April 29th ,1998 police officers came to my unit and I was at work then had me as a wanted subject based on the obviously racist complex false report. When I found out from a neighbor that the police had been looking for me, I immediately phoned them and allowed them to arrest me. After I allowed them to arrest me they improperly searched me for drugs (without a women officer present).The officers had no probable cause for a search. On or about September.14th 1998 case complant#98-20136 the officers did not even know what the charge was but that they had to make the arrest, I lost a days pay for this unprofessional behavior. (refer to County Complaint 98-7888).

On or about September14th 1998 officers again came to my apartment unit stating they needed to speak to my 17 yr old daughter,I told the officers that she was attending school at carl sandburg and that she was not here at the moment. The officers insisted that I was giving them false information so they insisted that they come in and see . I know if those officer were to come in my home I would lose my mind completely because due to the unfair treatment, I admitted myself into a close to home out patient mental health facility. On September 9th 1998 the medications the doctor put me on had not took it's full effect, upon their request to come in to my apartment was refused I stated you needed a search warrant, they replied"It's gonna take 3hrs to obtain one". I told them, to come back at that time. They refused and said they had to phone it in so they placed their foot in my door untill one officer phoned into the police station. Unprofessional behavior again as caused my family and I mental stress. (Refer to County Complaint #98-20136.The officers did not even know the charge.

On or about September. 23,1998 After trying all types of measures to plead with Mrs.Christine Peterson management of Sandburg Villiage apt, (Refer to King vs. A&Rkatz Sandburg Villiage #1:00-cv-01331 that due to the unfairness of her poor mananagement my mental health had began to fail me and asked if she could wait untill after our day in court which was October19th 1998. My mental health conselor phoned her as well. But this women (Christine Peterson) does not listen and entered my apt. while I was in the shower to do her inspection and was advised not to do so untill after our court date. She along with the Galesburg Police Department while I was naked the parties did go back into the hallway while my daughter threw me a gown to put on to cover my naked body but they insisted on coming in and they proceeded to come into my locked apartment and because we might have to move due to our pending eviction case on)October 19th 1998. We had our belongings in boxes the officers along with Christine Peterson Came in and started going threw our already packed belongings. They also got into my sons toys and fishing gear were they found a daisy BB.Gun and also in the box of fishing gear the found a fish cleaning knife and a long wooden stick that my son often plays baseball with they inproperly searched my unit gave false untrue statement on their police reports the officer did no mention how they arrested me with no undergarments and barefooted. I have witnesses who will testify under oath as to what really happened and due to my mental state of mind I did not know how to fight for my rights and took a guilty plea.
Not mentally secure in decision making at that time. On that same day of Sep 23rd 1998. While I was being arrested they sent a uni back out to arrest my 17yr old daughter on the charges that the did not know about on Sep.14th1998 . Each and every one of these

officers have lied about one thing or another sometime or another under oath in court and have also altered their police reports about my responses to the arrest slandered my character.I have people who will testify about my character . May 1998 (Refer to County Complaint) and April 7th 1999. Where I was physically, mentally and verbally abused as a result the judge found me guilty of as I feel defending myself against the officers but I was found mentally ill. How long will society go on ignoring the cries of the mentally ill when they kill the ones who contribute to there breakdown or untill they take their own lives before society sees a problem there was definetely a problem at sandburg village apartment complex the Galesburg police contribute to the problem instead of being fair and see the unstable pattern there at the complex the white tenants knew the law and worked their color of skin to make it work in thers favor .I chceked myself into the mental hospital I'm better now I will fight for my rights and claim money damages for my family and myself.

Respectfully Submitted
Mrs. Gwendolyn King

Mrs. Gwendolyn King

COMPLAINT # 78-8393 OFFICER HOSTENS 106 SANDROCK KN290

ON MAY 5, 1998 I TALISHA M. NICHOLSON ALONG WITH DASHAWN WATSON WITNESS FOR THE GOOD PART OF THE EVENING BEING HARASSED BY THE GALESBURG P.D. ON BEHAFE OF THE WHITE TEANTS IN THE COMPLEX WHERE WE ONCE RESIDED 676 HOME BLVD APT. 101 GALESBURG ILLINIOS. REFER TO CASE NO. 01911 KING V A &R KATZ . WHILE MY FAMILY AND FRIENDS WERE OUTSIDE ENJOYING THE NICE WHETHER BY HAVING A COOK OUT IT WAS LIKE THE NIEGHBORS COULD NOT STAND TO SEE MY FAMILY LIVE HAPPILY AND SINCE WE WERE THE ONLY BLACK FAMILY IN THE BUILDING THE NEVER TRIED TO REALLY GET TO KNOW US OR OUR CULTURE. THE WHITES IN OUR COMPLEX WOULD CALL THE POLICE AT 4, 5 O CLOCK IN THE AFTER NOON SAYING THAT WE WERE DISTURBING THEM THE POLICE WOULD COME OUT IN A VERY BAD UNPROFESSIONAL RACIST MANER THEY WOULD SHINE THEIR FLASH LIGHTS IN OUR FACE ALTHOUGH IT WAS STILL VERY LIGHT OUTSIDE, SHOUTING WHATS YOUR NAME! WE WOULD TELL THEM AND THEY WOULD SAY SOMETHING IN THE EFFECT THAT YOUR NIEGHBROS HAVE COMPLAINED AND WE ARE TELLING YOU TO KEEP IT DOWN! OR NEXT TIME WE WILL HAVE TO ARREST YOU NOT SAYING RATHER OR NOT THAT THERE WAS A DISTRUBANCE BUT THAT WE JUST BETTER KEEP IT DOWN AND INSPITE OF WHAT THEY (GALESBURG P. D.) SAY THEY NEVER ASK US OUR OPINION OR OUR VERSION OF WHAT HAPPEND AND WE COULD NOT BELIVE THAT THE TENANTS WOULD EVEN CALL AT THOSE TIME IN THE AFTERNOON 4,5,6,7 EVERYBODY ELES SEEM TO BE ABLE TO ENJOY THEIR PLACE OF RESIDENTS.

AFTER POLICE LEFT THE FIRST TIME 0N MAY 5, 1998 AT ABOUT 6 OCLOCK THEY RETURN SHORTLY ABOUT 7 OR 8 P.M. MY MOTHER GWENDOLYN NICHOLSON (KING)
WAS THE ONLY ONE OUTSIDE AT THE TIME ENJOYING HER PATIO AS SHE ALWAYS LOVED TO DO MY FAMLIY AND FRIENDS CAME INSIDE TO EAT OUR FOOD THAT WE JUST COOKED OUT
ON THE GRILL THE POLICE CAME BACK TO SAY THAT THEY RECIVED ANOTHER CALL STILL NOT SAYING THAT THERE WAS A DISTRUBANCE BUT TO JUST AGAIN KEEP IT DOWN AND IF THEY HAVE TO COME BACK THERE WILL BE AN ARREST. AT THAT TIME I TALISHA WENT TO TURN THE T. V. OFF MY MOTHER SAID FOR ME TO TURN THE T. V. BACK ON AND THAT WE HAD A RIGHT TO LIVE HERE WITHOUT BEING HARRASED. THEN I HEARD THE P.D. SAY NOT IF YOUR NEIGHBORS ARE COMPLANING. AFTER THAT STATEMENT WE KNEW THAT THE POLICE WAS NOT GOING TO BE FAIR AND TREAT US AS EQUAL WE JUST SAID OK OFFICERS.
AND THEY LEFT OUR FRIENDS AND FAMILY SLOWLY BEGAIN TO LEAVE . MY FRIEND KANDI CURTIS WAS THE LAST TO GET READY TO LEAVE . WE WENT OUTSIDE AT ABOUT I BELIVE IT WAS 9 O CLOCK WE HEARD HA! HA! NIGGER NOW LEAVE OR SOMETHING IN THAT EFFECT I KNOW IT WAS ALOT OF NIGGERS BEING CALL FROM INSIDE THE COMPLEX BUILDING .
BUT NOONE WOULD SHOW THEIR FACE. WE KANDI AND I CAME BACK INSIDE AND AT THAT TIME MY MOTHER HAD HAD IT AND DECIDED TO GO NEXT DOOR TO 103 APARTMENT.
I BELIVE IT MUST OF BEEN ABOUT 10 O CLOCK PM. WE KANDI , DASHAWN M. WATSON . AND MYSELF. HEARD MY MOTHER GWENDOLYN NICHOLSON (KING) SAY JUST LET ME TELL MY CHILDREN ! JUST LET MY CHILDERN ! AT THAT MOMENT I TALISHA NICHOLSON OPENED THE DOOR AND I SAW THE POLICE SHOVE MY MOTHER INSIDE THE DOOR WHERE THEY BEGAIN TO CHASE HER AROUND THE APARTMENT ALMOST STEPPING ON MY NEWBORN BABY AS THEY EVEN JUMPED OVER OUR COUCH THEY THEN GRABED MY MOTHERS ARM TWISTED IT AND GRABED HER BY THE NECK MY MOTHER WAS FRIGHTEN BY THE POLICE BEHAVIOR ALL EVENING

EXHIBIT

T. Nicholson Ex-1
V08/02   A6

83

THE POLICE AND THEIR BEHAVIOR HAD MY YOUNGER BROTHER AND I HAD BECAME
FRIGHTEN AS WELL. WE COULD NOT UNDERSTAND WHY THEY WOULD NOT ALLOW HER
TO TELL HER CHILDREN SHE WAS LEAVING WITH THEM , AS THEY CONTINUD TO
EXCESSIVELY ARREST MY MOTHER THEY HAD EVEN BEGAIN TO SHOVE ME TALISHA
NICHOLSON AROUND ASKING ME WHATS YOUR NAME! THEY FINALLY WAS ABLE TO
MAKE THE ARREST. ON THE WAY OUT TO THE POLICE CAR A HEARD MY MOTHER TELL
ME IN FEAR LOOK THE DOOR AND CALL FOR HELP! AND THATS WHAT I DID I CALLED MY
GRANDMOTHER LEE NICHOLSON . THE OFFICER DID COME BACK TO THE APARTMENT A
BANGED ON THE DOOR BUT MY BROTHER AND I WAS TO
FRIGHTEN TO ANSWER IT.
MY YOUNGER BROTHER IS AT THIS MOMENT IN A TRAMA STAGE. COME TO FINE OUT
LATER THAT THE WHITES IN THE COMPLEX PLACED A CALL SAYING MY MOTHER HAD
CHASED SOMEONE UP SOME STAIRS (NOT TRUE) BUT THE POLICE NEVER ASKED IF IT
WAS TRUE OR NOT BUT JUST CAME OUT TO ARREST MY MOTHER. THE WHITE PEOPLE
WHO OBVIOUSLY DID NOT LIKE FAMILY BECASUE WE WERE BLACK AMERICANS USED
THE COLOR OF THEIR SKIN AND THE LAW TO WORK THE SYSTEM. THE OFFICERS NEVER
DID INVESTIGATE INTO THE COMPLAINT.
THE SAME BEHAVIOR WAS DISPLAYED EXCEPT THERE WAS NO EXCESSIVE FORCE
WHICH BY THE WAY MY MOTHER ALLOWED THEM TO ARREST HER AND THAT WAS
BEFORE THE EXCESSIVE FORCE ARREST THATS WHY WE COULD NOT UNDERSTAND WHY
MY MOTHER WAS NOT ALLOWED TO TELL US SHE WAS BEING ARRESTED THAT MAY 5
1998 IT WAS I BELIVE APRIL 29 1998 THE POLICE HAD BEEN LOOKING FOR MY MOTHER TO
ARREST HER FOR A SO CALL DISTRUBANCE COMPLAINT NO. 9800248 BARRY D. HUFF #82
MY MOTHER AT THE TIME THEY HAD BEEN LOOKING FOR HER WAS AT WORK . WHEN MY
MOTHER AND I LEARNED THAT THE POLICE HAD BEEN LOOKING FOR HER BY ONE OF
HER FRIENDS I TALISHA PHONE THEM TO ASK THE NATURE OF THEIR VISIT . THEY SAID
THAT OFFICER HUFF HAS A SIGN COMPLAINT AND THAT THEY NEED TO ARREST
GWENDOLYN NICHOLSON I INFORMED MY MOTHER AS TO WHAT WAS SAID SHE SAID
TELL THEM TO COME ON BUT SHE NEEDED TO PHONE HER JOB AND SHE DID . UPON
THEIR ARRIVAL AFTER MY MOTHER ALLOWED THEM TO COME TO MAKE THE ARREST
WITHOUT EVEN KNOWING THE CHARGES THE GALESBURG POLICE ILEGALLY SEARCHED
MY MOTHER FOR DRUGS DID NOT EVEN TELL HER WHY SHE WAS BEING ARRESTED. IT
WASNT UNTIL SHE WAS IN THE HOLDING CELL THAT THEY SAID YOUR NIEGHBORS SAID
YOU DISTURB A MEETING . DID NOT ASK MY MOTHER OR I IF IT WAS TRUE BUT INSTEAD
SHE WAS THE ONE
WHO GOT ARRESTED.   *Continued from Pg 1*

3rd arrest

Holiday

ON MAY 24 1998 IT WAS IN THE AFTERNOON SOMETIME THEY COULD HEAR OUR T. V. ON
AND SINCE WE COULD NOT GO OUTSIDE TOO MUCH WE STAYED INSIDE ALOT THE
POLICE CAME AND SAID THAT OUR T. V. WAS TOO LOUD AND THAT WE NEED TO TURN IT
DOWN AND IF THEY GET ANOTHER CALL THERE WOULD BE AN ARREST MADE. WE
COULD NOT BELIVE THIS,
THE NIEGHBORS DID CALL ANOTHER ARREST WAS MADE
ANOTHER INCIDENT WERE THE WHITES LET IT BE KNOWN TO THE POLICE THAT WE
WERE NOT
WANTED AT THE COMPLEX WAS AT THE POOL ON JUNE 23 1998 THE POLICE WAS CALLED
AND THEY MADE MY FAMILY AND I LEAVE THE POOL FOR NO REASON, THAT UPSET MY
YOUNGER BROTHER TO TO POINT WERE HE DID NOT WANT TO GO OUTSIDE.

We, the residents of Sandburg Village Apartments, want Management
to evict Gwen Nicholson. We have heard that Management has
sent a termination of lease to Gwen and that she feels that
everyone is being prejudiced against her and she says that
this is why she is being evicted. This is not the truth.

The following residents want her gone because she has been
disturbing our rights, comfort and convience with her actions.
This has been going on for quite a while.

Area Code 309

672-103 Mona Anderson 344-2012
676-303 Sharii Shea 344-1208
674-107 Jean Huntley 344-2991
        Jennifer Ryle assigned
680-103 Lynn Hoyt none
676-202 Robert Huston 344-8219
        Barb Huston
678-107 Dorothy Foy none

        Virginia Kluska moved
668-103 Gene Kennedy 344-3977
        Dee Kennedy
        Brenda Brown moved
        Jim Brown
666-103 Sharon Palmer 342-2923
676-302 Mary Anderson 344-3193
670-105 Carol 342-8996
672-103 Tom Anderson 344-2012
674-102 Karen Sloan 343-5529
        now Karen Miner

Delona Kennedy
Gene Kennedy
684 Sherman Luallen 344-1562
701 Esther Luallen
704 Lou Kinsey 344-1633
680 Evelyn Boyd 344-1855
701

REC
6-1-98
CP

Bridgeway

Integrated Service Note

Service Date 2/28/00	Staff ID # 2945	Staff Name		
Appt. Time 1:45 PM	Time Spent :15	Location BI	Ghassan Bitar	
Individual Activity 126		Client Name		Client ID # 016653
Group Activity		Group Name	Gwendolyn King	
Progress Note:			G	Group ID #

Progress Note:

Patient presented today to the clinic. She was anxious and tearful. She reported that Buspar is not helping her anymore. She reported that she is not sleeping well at night. She denied suicidal or homicidal thought. At this point, because of the patient's complaints, I am going to discontinue Buspar and start patient on Paxil 20 mg one tablet at bedtime. I explained to her the possible side effects of Paxil. I provided her with a copy of Paxil's side effects. I will see the patient at her appointment scheduled on April 17, 2000. Patient is instructed to contact the clinic in case of any worsening of her symptoms.

Ghassan Bitar, M.D.
Staff Psychiatrist
Bridgeway, Inc.

CR86-2rev5/99

86

BRIDGEWAY

2-12-01

To whom it may concern

Ms. Gwendolyn King is one of my
patients, due to Mental illness
Ms King was not able to work
for the year 2000.
At Present she improved significantly
and she is planning to go back to
the Work face

G. Bilal MD
Ghassan Bilan   MD
Psychiatrist

BRIDGEWAY

Service Date	Staff ID #	Staff Name
02.29.00	2094	Anna M. Viviani

Appt Time	Time Spent	Location
04:00 AM/**PM**	01:00	Knox O.P.

Individual Activity
☑ 121 Individual therapy

Client Name: Deshawn Watson
Client ID # 022397

Group Activity
☐

Group Name:
Group ID # G

Progress Note:

Deshawn was accompanied by his mom. Mom joined us to talk about ITP. Both mom and Shawn signed it. Mom was very concerned about the effect of the discrimination on Shawn.

Shawn and I played one of the "feelings" games and drew. He stated he misses his friends from the old place and it isn't fair he can't go there to play - this is because mom isn't allowed on the property. We talked about discrimination and what he thinks. This came in after missing his friends and not having anything to do. He said there aren't as many friends to go outside with, so he plays video games/watches TV. Probably contributing to his weight gain. He is looking forward to summer and hopes to make some new friends to hang out c̄.

He agreed to talk more about his weight and self image issues next visit

Anna Viviani MA LPC QMHP
Staff Signature

CR86 - 2 rev 9/16/99

88

plates: of excessive force or Physical abuse.

May of 1998 (See County Complaint) I was Chased, Choked ~~tackled~~. arms twisted Pushed & Shoved.

Sept. 1998. (See County Complaint) was arrest without under garments no shoes arms were twisted Pushed and Shoved.

April 7 1999. (See County Complaint) Chased, Pushed, Choked arms twisted Slamed to the floor Causing my eye brow to be gashed. and Mace

Project: SANDBURG VILLAGE APARTMENTS
Contract: IL50H121008

Effective: 03/02/00
Printed: 03/02/00

Bldg/Unit	Last Name	Scheduled Effective	1999 First Reminder	1998 Second Reminder	1997 Third Reminder	1996 Tenant Response	95 94 93 92 91
01 666101	COLEMAN						
01 666102	RICHARDSON	08/01/00	W	W	W	W	
01 666103	BALMER	04/01/01	W	W	W	W	W W W W W
01 666104	MORROW	09/01/00		W	W	W	W W W W W
01 666201	BOWERS	07/01/00	H	H	W	W	W W W W W
01 666202	BELL	06/01/00	B	W	W	W	W W W W W
01 666203	NEEL	05/01/00	W	W	W	W	W W W W W
01 666204	HAYNES	08/01/00	W	W	W	W	B B B B W
02 668101	ADAMS	11/01/00	W	W	W	W	W W W W W
02 668102	FROST	12/01/00	W	W	W	W	W W W W W
02 668103	KENNEDY	07/01/00	W	W	W	W	W W W W W
02 668104	KINSEY	03/01/01	W	W	W	W	W W W W W
02 668201	WEEKS	10/01/00	W	W	W	W	W W W W W
02 668202	REYBURN	03/01/01	B	B	B	B	W W W W W
02 668203	LOCKE	09/01/00	W	W	W	W	W W W W W
02 668204	HANEGHAN	07/01/00	W	W	W	W	W W W W W
02 668301	CROWELL	09/01/00	W	W	W	W	W W W W W
02 668302	REA	08/01/00	B	B	W	W	W W W W W
02 668303	COBERT	05/01/00	W	W	W	W	W W W W W
02 668304	GRANT II	09/01/00	W	W	H	W	W B W W W
02 670105	LEE	06/01/00	B	W	W	W	W W W W W
02 670106	ENGLAND	03/01/01	W	B	B	B	B W W W W
02 670107	MCCOY	11/01/00	W	W	W	W	W W W W W
02 670108	DAHL	06/01/00	W	W	W	W	W W W W W
02 670205	ZIMMERMAN	11/01/00	W	W	W	W	W W W W W
02 670206	SPICHER	02/01/01	W	W	W	W	W W W W W
02 670207	BAILEY	10/01/00	W	W	W	W	W W W W B
02 670208	FORRESTER	07/01/00	W	W	W	W	W W W W W
02 670305	DUNHAM	10/01/00	W	W	H	W	W W W W W
02 670306	WILSON	11/01/00	W	W	W	W	W W W W W
02 670307	SWAIN	11/01/00	W	W	W	W	B B B W W
02 670308	MORSS	10/01/00	W	W	W	W	W W W W W
03 672101	HARRIS	01/01/01	W	W	W	W	W W W W W
03 672102	MORTON	11/01/00	B	W	B	B	B W W W B
03 672103	ANDERSON	09/01/00	W	W	W	W	B B B B B
03 672104	BLIXT	02/01/01	W	W	W	W	W W W W W
03 672201	COWAN	12/01/00	W	W	W	W	W W W W W
03 672202	BRACKEN	08/01/00	W	W	W	W	W W W W W
03 672203	SCOTT	10/01/00	W	W	W	W	W W W W W
03 672204	MASON	01/01/01	W	W	W	W	H W W W W
03 672301	FOX	04/01/01	B	W	W	W	W W W W W
03 672302	NAUGLE	03/01/01	W	W	B	B	B B B B W
03 672303	COOLEY	12/01/00	B	W	W	W	W W W W W
03 672304	ROGERS JR	02/01/01	W	W	W	W	W W W W W
03 674105	HAGGE	07/01/00	W	W	B	W	W W W W W
03 674106	ORTLIEB	12/01/00	W	W	W	W	W B R B W
		05/01/01	W	W	W	W	W W W W W

HUDManager 2000 v1.3.0 * (c) 1997-1999 by RealPage, Inc. * Tenant Report

ALL ANNUAL RECERTIFICATIONS REPORT Page 2 of 3

Project: SANDBURG VILLAGE APARTMENTS
Contract: IL50H121008

Effective: 03/02/00
Printed: 03/02/00

67 W
All white
and has been
for the years
I lived there
and W are harass…

Bldg/Unit	Last Name (Current 3/00)	Scheduled Effective	1999 First Reminder	1998 Second Reminder	1997 Third Reminder	1996 Tenant Response	95	94	93	92	91
03 674107	HUNTLEY W	04/01/01	W	W	W	W	W	W	W	W	W
03 674108	JOACHIM W	02/01/01	W	W	W	W	W	W	W	W	W
03 674205	BOYD W	12/01/00	W	W	W	W	W	W	W	W	W
03 674206	DUNCAN W	11/01/00	W	W	W	W	W	W	W	W	W
03 674207	BAILEY B	07/01/00	B	B	W	W	W	W	W	W	W
03 674208	PORTER W	07/01/00	W	W	W	W	W	W	W	W	W
03 674305	ENNIS W	07/01/00	W	B	B	B	W	W	W	W	W
03 674306	DAHL W	11/01/00	W	W	W	W	W	W	W	W	W
03 674307	RUTLEDGE W	11/01/00	W	W	W	W	W	W	W	W	W
03 674308	ROGERS W	12/01/99	W	W	W	W	W	W	W	W	W
04 676101	CENTENO W	07/01/00	W	B	B	B	W	W	W	W	W
04 676102	MINER W	05/01/01	W	W	W	W	W	W	W	W	W
04 676103	IBRAHIM W	06/01/01	W	W	W	W	W	W	W	W	W
04 676104	NELSON W	04/01/01	W	W	W	W	W	W	W	W	W
04 676201	DAMITZ W	10/01/00	W	W	W	W	W	B	B	B	B
04 676202	BERN W	03/01/01	W	W	W	W	W	W	W	W	W
04 676203	HUSTON W	02/01/01	W	W	H	W	W	W	W	W	W
04 676204	DEPPE W	12/01/00	W	W	W	W	W	W	W	W	W
04 676301	MINK W	03/01/01	W	H	W	W	W	W	W	W	W
04 676302	ANDERSON W	04/01/01	W	W	W	W	W	W	W	W	W
04 676303	SHEA W	11/01/00	W	W	W	W	W	W	W	W	W
04 676304	PETERSON W	11/01/00	W	W	W	W	W	W	W	B	W
04 678105	WILSON W	07/01/00	W	W	W	W	W	W	W	W	W
04 678106	MORRIS W	12/01/00	W	W	W	W	W	W	W	W	W
04 678107	FAY W	06/01/00	W	W	W	W	W	W	W	W	W
04 678108	THOMPSON W	07/01/00	W	W	W	W	W	W	W	W	W
04 678205	JOHNSON B	10/01/00	W	W	W	W	W	W	W	W	W
04 678206	EVANS W	09/01/00	W	W	W	W	W	W	W	W	W
04 678207	JOHNSON B	11/01/00	B	B	B	B	B	B	B	W	W
04 678208	HIGAREDA H	10/01/00	B	W	W	W	W	W	W	W	W
04 678305	SHEPHERD B	11/01/00	B	B	B	B	B	B	W	W	W
04 678306	STIMELING W	09/01/00	W	W	W	W	B	B	W	W	W
04 678307	HARRIS B	02/01/01	B	B	B	B	B	B	B	B	B
04 678308	COOPER W	06/01/00	W	W	W	W	W	W	W	W	W
05 680101	BOYD W	12/01/00	W	W	W	W	W	B	B	W	W
05 680102	PERDUE B/W	12/01/00	W	W	W	W	B	B	B	W	W
05 680103	HOPT W	11/01/00	W	W	B	B	W	W	W	W	W
05 680104	HENRY W	05/01/01	W	W	W	W	W	W	W	W	W
05 680201	LOPEZ H	12/01/00	H	W	W		W	W	W	W	W
05 680202	VANIER W	04/01/01	W	W	W	W	W	W	W	W	W
05 680203	MINER W	11/01/00	W	W	W	W	W	W	W	W	W
05 680204	COOLEY B	02/01/01	B	W	W	W	W	W	W	W	W
05 680301	HILLER W	10/01/00	W	W	W	W	W	W	W	W	W
05 680302	FULLER W	12/01/00	W	W	W	W	W	W	W	O	O
05 680303	JOHNSON W	09/01/00	W	W	W	W	W	W	W	W	W
05 680304	CRONKHITE W	11/01/00	W	W	W	W					

HUDManager 2000 v1.3.0 * (c) 1997-1999 by RealPage, Inc. * Tenant Report

O = Original

Project: SANDBURG VILLAGE APARTMENTS
Contract: IL50H121008

Effective: 03/02/00
Printed: 03/02/00

Bldg/Unit	Last Name	Scheduled Effective	1999 First Reminder	1998 Second Reminder	1997 Third Reminder	1996 Tenant Response	95	94	93	92	91
05 682105	CHURN W	10/01/00	W	W	B	B	B	B	B	B	B
05 682106	KILPATRICK W	02/01/01	W	W	W	W	W	W	W	W	W
05 682107	CARRICO W	04/01/01	W	W	W	W	W	W	W	W	W
05 682108	DANFORTH W	12/01/00	W	W	W	W	B	B	B	W	W
05 682205	HAYMON B	10/01/00	B	B	B	B	W	B	B	W	W
05 682206	PERKINS B	01/01/01	B	B	W	W	H	H	H	H	
05 682207	DUCKWORTH B	01/01/01	B	W	H	H	W	W	W	W	W
05 682208	WATSON B	02/01/01	B	W	W	W	B	B	B	B	B
05 682305	JACKSON B	03/01/01	B	B	B	B	W	W	W	W	
05 682306	LITTLE W	10/01/00	W	W	W	W	W	H	H	H	
05 682307	OLIN W	10/01/00	W	W	W	W	W	W	W	W	W
05 682308	GLADFELTER W	03/01/01	W	W	W	W	W	W	W	W	
06 684105	WASHINGTON B	08/01/00	B	B	W	W	W	H	H		
06 684106	BROWN W	02/01/01	W	W	W	W	W	W	W	W	W
06 684107	LUALLEN W	12/01/00	W	W	W	W	W	W	W	W	W
06 684108	CHAMBERS W	09/01/00	W	B	B	W	W	W	W	W	W
06 684205	PIERSON B	07/01/00	B	B	W	W	W	W	W	W	W
06 684206	HORMANN W	04/01/01	W	W	W	W	W	W	W	W	
06 684207	GROEL W	06/01/00	W	W	W	W	W	W	W	W	
06 684208	JACKSON B	12/01/00	W	B	B	B	B	B	W	W	W
06 684305	HAHN W	01/01/00	B	B	W	W	W	W	W	W	W
06 684306	ABARCA B	10/01/00	B	B	B	B	B	W	B	B	B
06 684307	SHREVES W	09/01/00	W	W	W	B	B	B	B	B	B
06 684308	BERN W	12/01/00	W	W	W	W	W	W	W	W	H
06 686101	LOUGH W	11/01/00	W	W	W	W	W	W	W	W	W
06 686102	MAXWELL W	10/01/00	W	W	W	W	W	W	W	W	W
06 686103	WALKER W	11/01/00	W	W	W	W	W	W	W	W	W
06 686104	ANDERSON B	12/01/00	B	B	B	B	W	W	W	W	W
06 686201	WARD B	05/01/00	B	H	H	H	W	W	W	W	W
06 686202	HARRIS B	04/01/00	B	B	W	W	W	W	B	B	B
06 686203	COATS B	08/01/00	B	B	B	B	B	B	W	W	W
06 686204	MELGOSA H	11/01/00	H	H	H	H	H	H	W	W	
06 686301	HERRING W	08/01/00	W	W	W	H	H	W	W	W	
06 686302	ALFARO H	10/01/00	H	H	H	H	W	W	H	H	H
06 686303	SENDERS W	11/01/00	W	W	W	W	W	W	W	W	W
06 686304	KELLEY W	11/01/00	W	W	B	B	B	B	B	B	B

92

Prophetess Final Words

Tearing down Satan's kingdom, I went through all that hell in life. Raised by the Holy Spirit himself for such a time as this! I pray that this book helps someone, that it would help heal the broken hearted pains of hurt. To let people know that everything that goes on in this world is not all of what it seems to be. Even though we have issues in our lives, we must become like the woman with the issue of blood (Luke 8:43) who suffered for twelve years but kept her faith strong. No matter how long we face an issue, we must press our way through the hurt of a bad relationship, press our way through a lost job, a foreclosed home! A repo car! Press your way through a drug habit! Press your way through all your issues and touch the savior of the world! The Lord Jesus Christ, the one who shed his blood for you to be healed! Be delivered! And be set free. Put your lives in the hands of God's Holy Spirit and you won't go wrong. Trust the lord, never doubt! He is your Lord and Risen Savior! He loves you, he died for you and he has already brought you out... IN JESUS NAME AMEN!!!!